GL🌍CAL

"In many respects, the Great Commission in the twenty-first century remains more a set of problems to be resolved than a task to be achieved. Rick Love both explains why the challenges exist and how to begin reconceiving Christian witness afresh. Some evangelicals will think he has gone too far in reconstructing mission, others will think he has not gone far enough in deconstructing it. It is precisely a book's capacity to elicit both kinds of responses that mark Glocal as a must-read for anyone with any stake in these issues in the present time."

—Amos Yong
Professor of Theology & Mission, Fuller Theological Seminary, Pasadena, CA

"All of those who 'follow Jesus' have to follow him in the real world. Today, questions and concerns abound. In this world of growing complexity, we need direction. We need guidance that will provide the wisdom and strength to love. This book does that. And it will make you wiser and bolder in love. Rick Love has the experience and expertise to pen this book."

—Tyler Johnson
Lead Pastor, Redemption Church AZ

"This is a book about integrity, meaning one who is the same in public as in private. Rick Love helpfully and so necessarily removes the masks that Christians wear in the Church, to Islam, and to the secular world, arguing that we must present the same face to all three, rather than one of subterfuge. It is a unique message that is so timely for this diverse and pluralistic world which has become increasingly Glocalized, and very few people prepare us for a time such as this like Love."

—Allen Yeh
Associate Professor of Intercultural Studies and Missiology, Biola University

"This book reflects Rick Love's wisdom from decades of international ministry experience. His heart for Jesus shines through in this very thoughtful examination of missions and missionary thinking. Rick uses his profound grasp of Scripture to illustrate a strategic way forward through the complexity of the interconnected world we live in. This is a must-read for young pastors, missions leaders, and anyone concerned about making disciples in the twenty-first century."

—Jay Pathak
Pastor, Mile High Vineyard; Co-author of *The Art of Neighboring*

"Globalization continues to bring disruption to Great Commission sending structures, especially in North America. Rick Love understands this new reality and speaks with a prophetic voice calling us to embrace authenticity and respect in the world of global engagement."

—Steve Moore
Executive Director, nexleader, ABHE; former President of Missio Nexus

"Have you ever experienced the satisfaction of hammering in a long nail while dangling from an awkward position and somehow hitting the nail smack in the middle with each blow? That's an apt analogy of how I felt as I turned each page of Rick's newest book: deep satisfaction from a theoretical, theological, and practical level. Followers of Jesus need a new paradigm for understanding themselves, the world, and our Muslim neighbors. This is it, or at least a piece of it."

—Scott Breslin
International Director of Operation Mercy

"Glocal is an essential read. Rick's telling of his pilgrimage from an evangelical mission leader to global peace catalyst bears lessons for all leaders desiring to be relevant today. Rick hones in on the need for both integrity and cohesion in our message, identity, and mandate. His passion to see the authentic Gospel embraced by all permeates the pages, especially by reminding us that people should be seen as neighbors not projects. . . . I believe this book will help liberate you to live wholly into your convictions with a clear and consistent identity, regardless of the audience, in our extremely interconnected world."

—John Becker
Director of Ministries, AIM International;
Founder, SOIL - Society of Intentional Lives

GL🌍CAL

Following Jesus in the 21st Century

Rick Love

CASCADE *Books* • Eugene, Oregon

GLOCAL
Following Jesus in the 21st Century

Copyright © 2017 Rick Love. All rights reserved. Except for brief quotations in critical publications or reviews, no part of this book may be reproduced in any manner without prior written permission from the publisher. Write: Permissions, Wipf and Stock Publishers, 199 W. 8th Ave., Suite 3, Eugene, OR 97401.

Cascade Books
An Imprint of Wipf and Stock Publishers
199 W. 8th Ave., Suite 3
Eugene, OR 97401

www.wipfandstock.com

PAPERBACK ISBN: 978-1-5326-0208-5
HARDCOVER ISBN: 978-1-5326-0210-8
EBOOK ISBN: 978-1-5326-0209-2

Cataloguing-in-Publication data:

Names: Love, Rick—1952.

Title: Glocal : Following Jesus in the 21st century / Rick Love.

Description: Eugene, OR: Cascade Books, 2017 | Includes bibliographical references.

Identifiers: ISBN 978-1-5326-0208-5 (paperback) | ISBN 978-1-5326-0210-8 (hardcover) | ISBN 978-1-5326-0209-2 (ebook)

Subjects: LCSH: Globalization—Religious aspects—Christianity. | Christian missions. | Title.

Classification: BR121.3 .L67 2017 (paperback) | BR121.3 (ebook)

Manufactured in the U.S.A.   06/20/17

Contents

Preface | vii

Part I: Introduction
1. Mother Jones, the Princess, and the Prince | 3
2. Following Jesus in a Glocalized World | 11
3. Paradigm Shifts and Heart Renewal | 25

Part II: A Core Message Worth Dying For
4. Jesus-Centered | 37
5. Jesus-Centered and Kingdom-Focused | 45

Part III: A Core Identity Worth Living For
6. An Integrated Identity | 57
7. Work, Worship, and Witness | 65
8. Paul the Businessman-Follower of Jesus | 72

Part IV: A Core Dream Worth Suffering For
9. Blessing All Nations | 83
10. Blessing and Human Rights | 92
11. Blessing and Peacemaking | 99
12. Blessing and Sharing the Gospel with Integrity: The Ethics of Evangelism | 105

Part V: Bearers of Blessing Among Neighbors and Nations
13. Aligning Ourselves with a Glocal World | 115
14. Starting a Glocal Reformation: Lessons Learned from Martin Luther | 121

Works Cited | 125

Preface

I am writing to foster a conversation with anyone concerned about being a faithful follower of Jesus and a winsome witness for Jesus: pastors, mission leaders, and young people just beginning to feel out their paradigms for ministry.

This book is part personal journey, part cultural analysis, but mostly an urgent call for a paradigm shift. I tell my story, so it includes personal experience and confession. I expose the new challenges of living out our faith in a radically interconnected world, so it includes prophetic critique. But both the personal and prophetic have one goal in mind: to help lead the church into a new paradigm.

And what is this new paradigm? I describe an approach to ministry that helps us live as faithful followers of Jesus in the midst of the religious, relational, political, and communicational complexities of the twenty-first century. Three far-reaching global trends—terrorism, pluralism, and globalization—have irrevocably altered how we live, think, and communicate in the twenty-first century. These three trends function as either barriers or as bridges for Christ, depending on *how* we respond to them.

We live in a "glocal" world: what happens globally impacts us locally, and what happens locally impacts things globally. What happens among the nations impacts our neighbors, and what happens among our neighbors impacts the nations. Thus, the term *glocalization* highlights the comprehensive connectedness of the world in which we live.

This story vividly explains what it means to live in a glocalized world:

> The Heartsong Church of Memphis, Tennessee, learned that the Memphis Islamic Center had bought the land adjacent to their church. They were faced with a choice. Would they see their new neighbors as a threat and react out of fear? Or would they choose to view this as an opportunity to be a witness for Christ?

Preface

Pastor Stone said on MSNBC, "As fast as we could . . . we put up a big red sign that said, 'Welcome to the neighborhood Memphis Islamic Center.'"

Dr. Bashar Shala, chairman of the Memphis Islamic Center responded: "You couldn't miss the sign. It was really a sign that gave us a lot of joy, a lot of comfort, and told us that we have neighbors that are welcoming us. And what followed the sign was even larger and more gracious in the actions of the Heartsong church [sic] towards our community."

While the Memphis Islamic Center was waiting for its building to be built, the Heartsong Church let the Muslim community use their church building during Ramadan, the Islamic month of fasting. They have shared thanksgiving [sic] dinner together and they plan to collaborate on building a community park using four acres from each community.

Meanwhile, Pastor Stone was asked to do an interview on *CNN International* regarding his hospitable relationship with his new neighbors during the time when Terry Jones, an American pastor, was receiving a lot of media attention for threatening to burn Qur'ans in protest of the possibility of an Islamic center being built near the site of the 2001 September terrorist attacks in Manhattan, New York.

When Pastor Stone's interview aired, a room full of Muslims on the other side of the earth in Kashmir watched in amazement. One Muslim man left the room without telling anyone where he was going. When he came back, they asked where he had been: "I went to the small Christian church down the road to clean it," he responded (in paraphrase).

Another Muslim man in the room who watched the interview spent four hours attempting to call Pastor Stone. When he finally got through to his church office phone in Memphis, the man said (in paraphrase): "It was like God was talking through you. Dr. Stone, please tell people in your country we are not terrorists. We are so moved by the kind and loving way you are treating your Muslim neighbors in America that we are going to take care of the Christian church in our community in Kashmir for the rest of our lives."

As we build lasting friendships with and extend the hospitality of Christ to our religious neighbors, let us be aware of how our local actions have global repercussions.[1]

---

1 Daneshforooz, *Loving our Religious Neighbors*, 234–35.

Preface

Living in a glocal world radically challenges our communication. It also challenges how we live out our faith. This book articulates the need for a change in our wording and a change in our being.

Evangelicals often talk about an incarnational approach to ministry. By this we mean that Jesus left heaven and entered into our world. He became flesh and dwelt among us to reveal God to us. In evangelical practice this usually means we immerse ourselves in our context. We learn the culture and customs of our context in order to communicate effectively. We meet people where they are at, in their world. An incarnational approach to ministry is a divinely inspired, brilliant communicational strategy.

But the incarnation is so much more. Jesus not only spoke powerfully into his context, he also embodied the love of God. He manifested profound humility and sacrificial service. At the heart of an incarnational approach is the heart. The incarnation reveals the heart of God and God's desire to transform the heart of humanity. We are called to manifest the real presence of Jesus to a broken, bleeding, and beautiful world.

Jesus reflected and exemplified what could be called "beautiful orthodoxy." He was full of grace and truth (John 1:14). Jesus was known as the teacher of truth and the friend of sinners (Matt 11:19; 22:16). He boldly confronted the Pharisees (Matt 23) and graciously demonstrated humility (Matt 11:29). He taught and modeled both exclusive truth claims (John 14:6) and inclusive love aims (Matthew 5:44).[2] Truth and beauty dance side by side in the life of Jesus.[3]

Thus an incarnational approach, as I use the term in this book, involves relevant communication and beautiful orthodoxy. We are sent to be good-news people in a bad-news world!

I write to you, pastors and mission leaders, because you guide God's people. You have inherited the ministry paradigms of previous generations, and you have a God-given responsibility to discern what he is doing now, and to lead his people into the twenty-first century. May God help you adapt to the new revolutionary trends shaping our planet.

I write to you, the younger generation, because you have inherited the world of the twenty-first century. It's the only world you know. You probably already feel that the paradigms of the past don't fit. You may not

---

2 See Love, *Peace Catalysts*, 87–88; 144–45 for more about exclusive truth claims and inclusive love aims.

3. *Christianity Today*'s editor, Mark Galli, came up with the term "beautiful orthodoxy." Managing Editor Katelynn Beaty reflected on its meaning in *Christianity Today* January/February 2015, 7

be guiding God's people yet, but you are still responsible to hear the voice of the Good Shepherd and to follow him. Ultimately, you will be the leaders of the future, so start now. Go for it!

PART I

Introduction

1

Mother Jones, the Princess, and the Prince

> Today we live in a media-saturated, Internet-connected, cell phone-equipped world in which everything that happens anywhere is instantly available everywhere.
>
> RICHARD STEARNS

In January of 2002, just a few months after 9/11, I taught a course at Columbia International University (CIU) called "Church Planting in the Muslim World." I was international director of Frontiers—a large mission focused on inviting all Muslims to follow Jesus. A freelance journalist named Barry Yeoman wanted to sit in on our class so he could write something about followers of Jesus in the Muslim world. He had fairly represented evangelicals in previous articles, so the administration of CIU and I decided to let him attend my class.

Barry was an eager student. He brought a Bible and looked up every verse I mentioned—and we spent much time in Scripture. I am sure he did more Bible study in that week than he had done in his whole life! (Barry was Jewish.) He also readily engaged the students at breaks and during meals.

In May 2002, I was shocked when his article came out in a magazine called *Mother Jones*. *Mother Jones* is an American independent news

Part I: Introduction

organization reporting on politics, the environment, human rights, and culture. It is reportedly one of the most widely read liberal publications in the United States.

The article made the front cover of the magazine. A picture of a fully veiled Muslim woman with a necklace and a cross hanging around her neck provided the background for the provocative title: "The Stealth Crusade." Wow! I was not happy about that.

I quickly turned to the article and found that Barry did a good job of describing the dynamics of the class and *some* of the content of the course. But the article claimed our explicit mission was to "wipe out Islam"—an outrageous and totally fallacious comment! Those fanatical words were never uttered in the class, nor did we portray that extreme, combative attitude.

Sharing the gospel and wiping out Islam are two radically different things. In fact, the class focused on being a positive witness for Jesus, not on attacking Islam. When I emailed Barry after the article was published, he admitted that I did not say some of the things mentioned in the article. He attributed them to certain students outside of class, so he felt justified in including them in the article.

I don't doubt that some zealous students might have said something like this, especially since this was right after 9/11. What I don't like is that it was attributed to me by association, and that it skewed the meaning of the entire article. Anyone reading the article could easily view the class through the lens of violent fanaticism—which is blatantly wrong. Nevertheless, I can understand why Barry might have interpreted my students' words this way. The use of militant language is unfortunately a problem among evangelicals, which I address in the chapter "Paradigm Shifts and Heart Renewal."

Yeoman overstated and exaggerated what was said in class. He was, after all, a journalist trying to make a splash. But he did his homework, and I must confess that many aspects of his article exposed a lack of biblical breadth and depth in evangelical paradigms and practices. His public "exposé" contained enough truth to be embarrassing. While I forthrightly disagree with his embellishment, the good parts of his article forced me to reevaluate some of my beliefs and practices in light of Scripture. That's why I had to write this book.

The story in *Mother Jones* and the ensuing response also powerfully displayed how different the world had become since 9/11. In the past, only a liberal audience in the US would have read this article. But because of globalization, this article ricocheted throughout the world. It was published by *Utusan Melayu* (Malaysia), *Nawa-i-Waqt* (Pakistan), *UmmaNews* (international wire), *The Independent* (United Kingdom), *Payvand* (Iran), *Ottawa Citizen* (Canada), and *Weekend Australian* (Australia), to name a few.

A friend of mine who lived in Pakistan told me how he felt when the *Mother Jones* article was published in his country. He basically did not want to be associated with me anymore. He said he actually practiced saying in the local language, "I don't know Rick Love!"

Soon afterward I was asked to be interviewed by:

- *National Geographic Channel* (United States)
- *The Washington Post* (United States)
- *Christianity Today* (United States)
- *The New York Times* (United States)
- *CNN International*
- *National Public Radio* (United States)
- *60 Minutes* (Australia)
- *Courrier International* (France)
- *September Films* (United Kingdom)
- *60 Minutes II* (United States)
- *Der Spiegel* (Germany) and
- *talkSPORT* radio (United Kingdom).

I said "no!" to these interviews. I didn't want to share in a high-profile way about our work in Muslim countries. Moreover, evangelical mission leaders generally don't do interviews with the secular press, especially in response to such a negative article.

Our interconnected world had confronted me with a vengeance. I felt exposed as the full force of living in a globalized world hit me. I wasn't just unaware and caught off guard; I was oblivious to these global realities. To be honest, the whole evangelical missions world—of which I was a prime representation and example—was blind to the impact of globalized media.

Basically, those of us working in missions didn't know how to engage the press. We thought we could live and communicate in two separate worlds. We were operating as if there was no connection between our in-house conversations with fellow Christians, and our conversation with

Part I: Introduction

those outside the household of faith. It was like we were speaking two different languages—one to "insiders" and another to "outsiders." This didn't cause us discomfort when our two worlds remained separate, but when the Internet ambushed us with a new "one-world reality," we were forced to confront this duality.

A WHOLE NEW WORLD

Barry Yeoman sensationalized the topics and conversations in my class. But why not? Muslims were *the* hot topic after 9/11. What was taught privately in a Christian university could now be publically proclaimed among the nations. What was once a low-profile, boring topic became high-profile news.

A few years after the *Mother Jones* article, I attended the National Prayer Breakfast in Washington, D.C. I hung out with the Middle East delegation and made many new Muslim friends. I remember sitting with a prince and princess from the Middle East during a meal. When I introduced myself, the princess said, "Rick Love . . . I have heard about you!" With the recent article on "The Stealth Crusade" fresh in my mind, I got nervous and shot back quickly (but respectfully), "Don't believe everything you read!" She smiled and then we both turned our attention to another conversation that was going on.

I shared this incident with a wise friend of mine. He knew about the *Mother Jones* article and talked to me about my interaction with the princess. He said, "Rick, you need to set up your own website." I said, "No way! It's really egotistical to have your own website." His response stunned me: "Rick, either you define yourself, or someone else will." That event helped birth my approach to communication in a globalized world. Ricklove.net soon found its way among the millions of websites vying for hits in a Google-ized world.

But back to "The Stealth Crusade."

We evangelicals face a daunting communication problem. How we have talked about those outside the church does not communicate well to a twenty-first-century audience. But to be honest, we have more than just a communication problem. At the root of our communication problems are integrity issues. Feelings of self-righteousness and judgment too often lurk in our hearts. Pride and contempt hide just beneath the surface. And these heart issues seep into our communication. They were there all along, but our evangelical tribal triumphalism muffled our conscience. We have not dealt with these deeper issues because we thought that the way we do things was the only possible way we could obey Jesus. And when I say "we," I include myself. I had a lot to learn.

The *Mother Jones* article launched me on a pilgrimage of profound reflection and introspection about how we communicate and live out the gospel in a glocalized world. It made me evaluate my motivation, my message, my mandate, and my method like never before.

RETHINKING THE HEART OF COMMUNICATION AND THE INTEGRITY OF THE HEART

In 2005 I went on a three-day spiritual retreat. I spent my time praying, fasting, reading Scripture, and reflecting on the challenges of following Jesus in a glocalized world. By the end of the third day, I was convinced that God was calling me to something new. At that time I was calling it "3D"—shorthand for three-dimensional communication—because it involved communicating one core message to three audiences (Christian, Muslim, and secular) simultaneously. I sensed I heard God's voice, and I was determined to lead people into a new paradigm of life. I began pursuing what it meant to live out the gospel with wisdom, integrity, and boldness in a glocalized world.

In 2007 I realized that with this new calling I could no longer serve as international director of Frontiers. While grateful for the gifted colleagues and rich friendships I enjoyed in Frontiers, I felt I needed to step down from my role to pioneer a new way of engaging those outside the church. It was time for me to search the Scripture and my soul, and to reevaluate many things I once held dear.

The aftermath of 9/11 didn't just expose the church's weaknesses at engaging those outside the church. It also ignited a new fire in me. I experienced a transformation that broadened and deepened my commitment to peacemaking. Prior to 9/11, I focused on interpersonal peacemaking between followers of Jesus.

Now I felt called primarily to peacemaking outside the church—intergroup peacemaking, especially between Christians and Muslims.

So I went on a sabbatical at Yale University to do research at the Yale Center of Faith and Culture's Reconciliation Program.

Part I: Introduction

I was hungry to read, research, and reflect on what peace and reconciliation meant in a multi-religious world in conflict.

But that reflective, research sabbatical was not to be. Something much more amazing took place. On October 13, 2007, 138 influential Muslim clerics, representing every school and sect of Islam from around the world, wrote an open letter to Christians everywhere calling for dialogue based on the common ground of "love of God and neighbor." This open letter was called "A Common Word." One of the first and most high-profile responses to this call for dialogue was issued by the Yale Center for Faith and Culture's Reconciliation Program, which in turn resulted in a global conference at Yale University in July of 2008.

I was asked to recruit Christian leaders to sign the Yale Response and to help put on the conference at Yale. Instead of studying about peacemaking, I got a chance to learn practically during my sabbatical. I did do some research, but most of my time was spent preparing for the Common Word Conference at Yale.

In preparation for the conference I was in email correspondence with many high-level Muslim leaders from around the world. One of the emails from a prince in the Middle East ended with this postscript: "Are you the same Rick Love of Frontiers and 'Stealth Evangelism'? When did you come to Yale?"

I reeled and felt sick to my stomach! I had spent six years wrestling with how to be free from stealth evangelism. Did this mean that I would be falsely perceived as the guy who wanted to wipe out Islam? What a painful email. I was hoping to begin a new future, but I couldn't escape my past. After talking this over with a few key friends and praying a lot, I responded:

Dear Prince _____,

Thank you so much for your prompt response and wise counsel. I am honored that your Royal Highness wants to participate. The list of leaders you suggested is impressive indeed. As you recommend, we will wait until people arrive to invite them.

Yes, I am the Rick Love of Frontiers, though I believe I was misrepresented in the article you mentioned. Nevertheless, that article launched me on a pilgrimage of reflection about the ethics of *da'wa* and evangelism, and I am no longer the person I was then. I stepped down from my role as international director of Frontiers at the end of 2007 because I feel as though God is calling me to spend the next phase of my life being a peacemaker between Muslims and Christians, and challenging my fellow Christians to be more ethical towards Muslims.

I am currently on sabbatical as a fellow of the Yale Reconciliation Program where I have been working hard to facilitate the upcoming Common Word Conference.

Re: "Stealth Evangelism" . . . I never said some of the outrageous and provocative things mentioned. Sadly, the author twisted facts and misrepresented Christian attitudes. I am sure you have experienced how the press can distort things for their own purposes. Having said that, there is clearly room for improvement. In the last few years I have been seeking to encourage Christians to find better ways to honestly talk about our faith with Muslims. That's why I look forward to meeting with you for honest discussion during the Common Word Conference.

Salam,
Rick

The prince's response was a huge encouragement:

Dear Dr. Rick,

Thank-you for that clarification; Indeed, the answer to my question is "no," you are not the same Rick Love, is it not? Lol.

I feel a lot of blessing and humility in your writing—indeed we are all familiar with the *Mother Jones* article; but we are also familiar with your considered defense of monotheism in the open discussion with John Piper. . . .

Wow! The prince had a sense of humor! He also carefully searched the Internet to learn about me and anything related to the Common Word. Thankfully, John Piper had graciously posted my response to his critique of the Common Word on his website. And I am glad that my response to John was informed by the *Mother Jones* fiasco. I wrote every word of that response imagining a Muslim and a secular journalist reading over my shoulder, in order to make sure that I would not be misunderstood by either group.

Part I: Introduction

Mother Jones, the princess, and the prince. These three encounters rocked my world and birthed this book. They led me to see my life and ministry in a radically new light.

2

Following Jesus in a Glocalized World

> The whole world has gone glocal!
> BOB ROBERTS JR.

I recall the first time it dawned on me how "glocal" the world really was. I was in Bahrain having dinner with a Bahraini colonel and his family in the late 1990s when I was US Director of Frontiers. We were drinking tea after the meal when the colonel told me that his son attended a university in the US. I remember commenting, "What a small world we live in!" Then I remembered that Frontiers had just set up its website and my picture had been posted on it. The thought of this Muslim colonel's college student finding my picture online caused me to break into a cold sweat. The next day, I had my IT guy take my picture off the site. This was the first of many instances where the missionary paradigm of having two "identities"—being a missionary in the US and a business coach outside the States—collided with a glocalized world. I didn't like it, but at that point I didn't know what to do. (Most Muslim, Hindu, and Buddhist countries, and even some secular ones, don't provide missionary visas, so other avenues of work need to be found by prospective missionaries.)

Part I: Introduction

I can freely write about these awkward encounters now because they are part of my past. Incidents like these won't happen again, since I now enjoy an integrated identity (we'll talk a lot about that later).

Here's a vivid negative example of what it means to live in a glocal world. In September 2011, Florida pastor Terry Jones threatened to commemorate 9/11 by burning Qur'ans. News of this ricocheted around the world, causing uproar among Muslims locally and globally, drawing the attention of General David Petraeus, Defense Secretary Robert Gates, and even of President Barack Obama. These leaders convinced Jones not to follow through on his plan.

Sadly, six months later, Jones did in fact burn a Qur'an. The result? Mobs in Afghanistan, incited by the burning of the Qur'an, attacked a UN compound in Mazar-e Sharif, killing seven UN employees, and protests in Kandahar killed nine and injured more than ninety.

How could the pastor of a church with less than fifty members capture the attention of the world? Why was this such "hot" press? Glocalization! Jones's Qur'an burning, with the worldwide furor it incited, highlights the interconnectedness of the world.

Much of this book focuses on paradigms. I critique old models of missions in light of global trends and suggest new ways of following Jesus among our neighbors and among the nations. Glocalization demands new paradigms of ministry. Glocalization provides new keys to fruitfulness. Glocalization offers a key to following Jesus in the twenty-first century.

After more than a decade of reflecting on these issues, I realize that living in a glocalized world can be summarized in three groupings of three: *three global trends*—terrorism, pluralism, and globalization—result in the need to speak one message to *three audiences*—Christian, secular, and Muslim (or any other religious identity)—about *three aspects of our faith*—our message, our identity, and our global dream. This is such a mouthful, I often summarize this under the rubric of "3D" (three dimensions).

Before I give a detailed analysis of 3D, I want to reflect a moment on what it means to be faithful followers of Jesus and winsome witnesses for Jesus.

Jesus said, "Come, follow me, and I will show you how to fish for people!" (Matt 4:19, NLT). A command and a promise. Following and fishing. Instead of living by fishing, his followers will live to enlist others in kingdom life and adventures. This verse integrates two dynamics of discipleship: we follow, and we witness (see also Mark 1:17; Luke 5:1–10).

Following Jesus in a Glocalized World

The call to follow Jesus puts the emphasis on relationship and obedience. Following portrays the role of the learner. It is daily and dynamic. Jesus began his ministry by calling Peter to follow him, and Jesus ended his ministry by calling Peter to follow him (Matt 4:19; John 21:19, 22). Jesus said, "If any want to become my followers, let them deny themselves and take up their cross *daily* and follow me" (Luke 9:23, emphasis mine).

True believers follow. Daily. I have been following Jesus over forty years. I have experienced countless spiritual highs and ministry breakthroughs. I have also endured many tough times. I have found that following Jesus is always challenging, never boring. As we follow, something happens both in us and through us. Jesus transforms us into his image and extends his kingdom through us. What an adventure!

Following Jesus means we embrace an incarnational approach to our witness. The incarnation is the most spectacular instance of contextualization in history. God entered our world in Jesus to communicate his love. He took the initiative; he adapted; he lived among us and used human language to communicate to us—the greatest example of bridge-building communication in history!

But incarnational ministry is more than a paradigm for communicating the gospel; it is a way of living. The Apostle Paul describes it in terms of humble service.

> Do nothing from selfish ambition or conceit, but in *humility* regard others as better than yourselves. Let each of you look not to your own interests, but to the interests of others. Let the same *mind* be in you that was in Christ Jesus, who, though he was in the *form of God*, did not regard equality with God as something to be exploited, but *emptied himself*, taking the *form of a slave*, being born in human likeness. And being found in human form, he *humbled himself* and became obedient to the point of death—even death on a cross. Therefore God also highly exalted him and gave him the name that is above every name, so that at the name of Jesus every knee should bend, in heaven and on earth and under the earth, and every tongue should confess that Jesus Christ is Lord, to the glory of God the Father (Philippians 2:3–11, emphasis mine).

The incarnation is not merely descriptive of what God has done in Christ; it is prescriptive for Jesus' followers. It is a paradigm for the Christian life: "let the same mind be in you that was in Christ Jesus" (v. 5). And what does the mind of Christ entail? Jesus emptied himself and humbled himself, modeling servanthood and dying on the cross. The downward trajectory is stunning: from God, to human, to slave, to crucified criminal. The incarnation is the greatest example of humility and servanthood the world has seen. The God of the universe is humble and serves us. We are commanded to imitate his mind-set—the mind-set of radical humility and sacrificial service.

Faithful followers and winsome witnesses imitate the incarnation. We adapt or contextualize to these new global trends and communicate accordingly. We embody the mind-set of Jesus displayed in the incarnation by demonstrating humility and servanthood.

Incarnational ministry shapes both our way of communicating and living.

SHIFT HAPPENS: TERRORISM, PLURALISM, AND GLOBALIZATION

Three massive global trends—terrorism, pluralism, and globalization—have irrevocably altered how we live, think, and communicate in the twenty-first century. These trends can function as barriers—like the story of Terry Jones—or bridges—like the story of the Heartsong Church. Personally, I believe these three global shifts taking place today have some parallels with how God prepared the way for the church in the first century.

Paul the apostle said, "But when the fullness of time had come, God sent his Son" (Gal 4:4). Biblical scholars have interpreted the phrase "fullness of time" as denoting the many ways God literally paved the way for the spread of the gospel. Rome had built an excellent network of roads crisscrossing the Roman Empire, making travel reasonably safe and easy. The translation of the Old Testament into Greek (known as the Septuagint) and the use of Koine Greek (*koine* means "common," referring to the language of the street) were two other factors that facilitated a broader response to the gospel of Jesus.

In the present, God is paving new roads for the gospel. Global trends provide new opportunities for personal growth and new avenues for bearing witness. We need to see the hand of God in the glove of circumstances.

Because I have spent over thirty-five years in close relationships with Muslims, most of my illustrations are about Muslims. However, as I hope to demonstrate, the principles described and practices suggested have relevance for all ministry in the twenty-first century. They also have relevance for people not in Christian ministry including Muslims, Hindus, Buddhists, and anyone else concerned about integrity and good communication.

TERRORISM: THE SHIFT HITS THE FAN

The horrific terrorist attacks of 9/11 have deeply marked this generation. The proliferation of further terrorist strikes around the world and the rise of ISIS have given Muslim terrorists a high profile on the global stage. Because of this, Muslims of all stripes (not just the radical fringe of terrorists) are front-page news every day. This media attention frequently results in Islamophobia—prejudice against or an irrational fear of Muslims. In addition, Westerners who live in the Muslim world are of interest to the secular press. Before 9/11, few people outside church circles were interested in knowing what Christians were doing in the Muslim world. But now, anyone living and working among Muslims is of interest.

Terrorism has also raised the stakes of being publicly known as a Christian witness to Muslims in Muslim lands. People seen as "missionaries" (whether they are or not) are no longer just at risk of being expelled from Muslim countries by their governments. Now they may be intentional targets of violent extremists who claim to be Muslim.

I remember an email I received from a friend of mine who leads a Christian aid organization in the Middle East. He wrote: "We've had *fatwas* issued against us calling for our death; we've had suicide bombers arrested plotting to get us and had others try to sell us out to Iranian intelligence; we've had our house "bugged" and broken into; we've had spies infiltrate our employment ranks; and we've chosen to hold meetings with known t3rrorists [*sic*] in pursuit of God's peace." A short time after I got this email, a similar scenario took place in another country. But this time there were no threats, just violence. Joel Shrun was gunned down by an Al Qaeda group in Yemen on March 18, 2012. He was accused of proselytizing. Things are different in a post-9/11 world.

PLURALISM: THE SHIFT OF COLORS AND CREEDS IN OUR NEIGHBORHOODS

The second trend, pluralism, has two meanings. It can refer to theological pluralism—"all religions lead to God"—or cultural pluralism, which focuses on social diversity. I use the term here in the cultural sense. It describes

Part I: Introduction

the coexistence of people from diverse ethnic, religious, and political backgrounds within one society. Urbanization (the movement of people from rural areas to cities) and immigration (the movement of people between nations) have been major factors in the rise of pluralism. I like how Martin Marty describes it: pluralism is "what people opt to *do* with the fact of diversity."[1]

In Europe, some public communicators use inflammatory and derogatory terms like "Eurabia" and "Londonistan" to highlight the influx of Muslim people into their societies. Such terms reflect at best an unrealistically fearful perspective, and at worst, racism, both of which I strongly oppose. Nevertheless, the terms vividly describe the pluralism of Europe. We live in an increasingly multi-religious, multicultural, mobile world!

I was talking with my friend Pastor Jamie Wilson about the changes in San Diego in the last two decades. I was shocked to hear of the radical demographic shifts in the city. Here are some of the facts he shared:

- In 1990, every zip code in San Diego was majority white. Today San Diego (the eighth largest city in America) is 32 percent Hispanic (with many areas that are majority Hispanic), 12 percent Asian American, 5 percent African American, and 13 percent other.
- The University of California at San Diego has gone from the whitest of all the UC schools in 1990 to a school where the freshman class is over two-thirds Asian American and the student population as a whole is twenty-four percent Caucasian (2011 number).
- Asian Americans are the fastest growing ethnic group by percentage right now.
- A large mosque was recently completed and another new mosque is in the works. The Muslim community in San Diego is growing very rapidly, and, according to Wikipedia, there are now 100,000 Muslims in San Diego.

I remember the surprise I experienced walking down the street where I once lived in Arizona, when a young Muslim girl walked out of one of the houses wearing a *hijab* (a Muslim head covering). The color and creed of our neighborhoods are changing.

Coca-Cola ran an ad for the 2014 Super Bowl celebrating America's diversity. A beautiful rendition of "America the Beautiful" was sung in

---

1. Marty, *When Faiths Collide*, 70.

English, Tagalog, Spanish, Hebrew, Hindi, Keres, and Senegalese-French. I was deeply touched, but many Americans reacted negatively.

I understand that everyone struggles with diversity at some level. We don't like certain beliefs or lifestyles. But diversity is a fact of life in the twenty-first century. According to Diana Eck, professor of comparative religions at Harvard, "The United States has become the most religiously diverse nation on earth."[2]

In the not-too-distant past, the evangelical view of the world was neatly divided into sending countries and mission fields. This is no longer the case. The mission fields of the past (Latin America, Africa, and Asia— also described as the Global South) are now sending nations. Moreover, significant populations coming from countries with little or no exposure to the gospel (referred to as "unreached peoples" by evangelicals) now live in Western nations that have historically been missionary-sending countries. Of course, the nearness of these peoples presents a wonderful opportunity to bear witness to Christ. It is no longer accurate to divide the world into sending nations and mission fields. Jesus' words are even more relevant today: "the [mission] field is the world" (Matt 13:38).

However, that same proximity produces challenges regarding the missionary's identity. In restricted-access countries, many cross-cultural Christian workers live with dual identities. They are recognized as missionaries by sending churches at home, but in their adopted homelands and by secular audiences, they are known by the type of work they do. When the world was less pluralistic, the two identities remained separate and clear. But as societies intermingle, these workers begin to experience a kind of spiritual schizophrenia that can undermine integrity and rob workers of joy and boldness.

GLOBALIZATION: THE SHIFT MAKES US GLOCAL

Globalization is a massive and complex phenomenon, a genuine revolution. I like George Rupp's two-sentence summary: globalization "entails increasingly efficient transfers of money, goods and services, and ideas across every sort of social and cultural border. It puts us more frequently, more rapidly and more intensely in contact with others all over the world."[3] Mark

---

2. Eck, *A New Religious America*, 4.
3. Rupp, "Sending, Receiving, Embracing," 23.

Part I: Introduction

L. Russell also describes globalization memorably. He argues that globalization is driven by the "three ITs": information technology, inexpensive travel, and international trade.

Globalization is not slowing down! In C-SPAN's January 19, 2012 episode of *US Conference of Mayors*, Thomas Friedman spoke about the world moving from a connected world to a hyper-connected world. Friedman exclaimed, "When I wrote *The World is Flat* in 2005, there was no Facebook. Twitter was just a sound; the Cloud was still up in the sky; 4G was a parking spot; Apps were what you sent to get a job; and Skype was a just typo."[4]

Today we acknowledge one indisputable reality: globalization means that the world is just a mouse click or a touchscreen tap away. Perhaps the most powerful and relevant example of this is the Internet search engine Google. In our "Google-ized" world, whenever we describe who we are, what we do, or why we do it, our words move quickly beyond our intended audience and enter the global marketplace of ideas. Private communication often becomes public knowledge, whether we like it or not! Alan Cohen says, "Google is like God. God is wireless, God is everywhere, and God sees everything. Any questions in the world and you ask Google."[5] Add to this Facebook, LinkedIn, blogs, YouTube, and Twitter, and the opportunities to communicate for good or evil are breathtaking.

Here's an example that illustrates the profound challenges of living in a "Google-ized" world. In 2006, *Chicago Tribune* reporter John Crewdson wrote an article about the accessibility of "secret" information. He searched a commercial online data service that supplied a directory of more than 2,600 CIA employees. One of the world's premier undercover organizations was "outed" by a simple online search! His article concludes: "Only recently has the CIA recognized that in the Internet age its traditional system of providing cover . . . is fraught with holes, a discovery that is said to have 'horrified' CIA Director Porter Goss."[6]

If this happens to the CIA, how much more likely is this to happen among evangelicals living in restricted-access countries? Followers of Jesus in restricted-access countries usually procure secure email, encrypt their computers, develop a long list of code words, and spend anxious moments thinking about the possibility of being outed as a missionary. I see three options for the future. They can continue with the same approach and let their

---

4. Friedman, "Thomas Friedman Remarks to U.S. Conference of Mayors."
5. Friedman, *The World is Flat*," 159.
6. Crewdson, "Internet Blows CIA Cover."

anxious moments increase. They can "out" themselves and call themselves missionaries (or some comparable term—pastor, priest, theological professor, etc.). Or they can dig more deeply into the Scriptures, think more carefully about the new world order, and reflect more personally about their own gifts, personality, and calling in order to discern a new paradigm of ministry.

Timothy Tennett, president of Asbury Theological Seminary, has written about "Being a 'Glocal' Preacher." He points out that "today the forces of globalization have created a new situation where there is no such thing as a mere local context. Today, every local context is informed by the larger global context. In short, whether we like it or not, we preach within the larger context of globalization."[7]

Bob Roberts Jr., a Southern Baptist pastor of a megachurch, writes about glocal ministry in his innovative book, *Glocalization: How Followers of Jesus Engage a Flat World*. Instead of putting on a traditional missions conference in his church, Roberts hosts global faith forums that he calls "From a Conversation about Other Faiths to a Conversation with Other Faiths." He invites several religious leaders, including Muslims and Jews, to speak to his church. (I had the privilege of speaking there in 2014.) As a Southern Baptist, Roberts remains passionate about the Great Commission and uncompromising regarding the gospel. But he also fervently models the Great Commandments (love of God and neighbor) and demonstrates deep respect for those outside the church. Roberts is creatively reimagining the nature of the church's global vision.

This doesn't just relate to preachers. Leaders in my own field—peacemaking and conflict resolution—also describe the adjustment they have made to these new glocal realities. Speaking of life in a post-9/11, globalized world, Oliver Ramsbotham, Tom Woodhouse, and Hugh Miall point out the dynamic synergy between local and global conflicts. Local conflicts manifest themselves globally, and global conflicts manifest themselves locally. Because of this, they have coined a new term, "'cosmopolitan conflict resolution' . . . an approach . . . which promotes constructive means of handling conflict at local through to global levels in the interests of humanity."[8]

Terrorism, pluralism, and globalization challenge us to live and communicate with greater wisdom and integrity. If we adjust to these trends, the potential for kingdom influence increases, and opportunities for Christ

---

7. Tennett, "Being a 'Glocal' Preacher."
8. Ramsbotham et al., *Contemporary Conflict Resolution*, 250.

multiply. If we fail to adjust, our message will be misunderstood, our ministry will be hindered, and our own souls risk being tainted by duplicity. Some Christians who choose to live and share Jesus in other countries and cultures may unnecessarily be put at risk of expulsion, persecution, or even death.

Perhaps a look at one particular word can illustrate the challenge of communicating and living in a world shaped by globalism, terrorism, and pluralism. Churches have become accustomed to hearing that they shouldn't use the word *missionary* in print for someone living in a restricted-access country. But most churches (and perhaps many missionaries) misunderstand the reasons why. They think the entire issue centers around "security." They don't want their people kicked out of the country. But the issue has as much to do with meaning as it does security.

To evangelical church members, and initially to cross-cultural workers themselves, the word *missionary* refers to someone who is compelled by Christ's love to give up family and friends and to move to a different culture to share the good news of Christ. But to the secular world, the word *missionary* refers to someone who arrogantly assumes they know better than everyone else. These missionaries are driven to proselytize otherwise happy and innocent people who would be better off without religious conflicts being introduced.

How do Muslims understand the term *missionary*? Since colonialism coincided with missionary activity throughout Asia, the Middle East, Africa, and Latin America, Muslims understand a missionary to be someone who moves to their country with imperialistic motives. They have come to attack Islam and impose their faith. Missionaries have a hidden agenda to Christianize them, often through financial or economic incentive. Their activities then pave the way for Western ideas, immoral lifestyles, and at times foreign governments, to conquer their lands and people. Obviously, missionaries do not aspire to be arrogant, intolerant, fanatical bearers of religious conflict. They want to represent Jesus, not their home country's government, and they are discouraged when they learn how they are perceived.

I think John Borelli rightly describes the communicational challenge of the word *missions* (and by association *missionary*): "The word 'mission' functions in the same way among Muslims as the word 'jihad' does among Christians. Both are beautiful words [to their respective faith communities], but in their use or perceptions there are implications of violence which are difficult to avoid." We need to find new language to communicate effectively in the twenty-first century.

PROBLEMS AND NEGATIVE CONSEQUENCES OF OLD PARADIGMS IN A GLOCALIZED WORLD

In light of the different meanings that words (like *missionary*) can communicate, the following examples of life in a glocalized world demonstrate the pain and problem of dual identities.

- A Christian professor with a PhD in history lives in the Middle East. He has worked hard to lecture with excellence and serve with integrity as a professor. One day, he searches his own name on the Internet and is shocked and disheartened to find himself described as a missionary. A well-meaning church where he had spoken posted their Sunday bulletin on their website.
- A family living with a work visa in a Southeast Asian Muslim country returns to the US for a visit. They are invited to an international student's concert, sponsored by their home church. Some students from the family's Southeast Asian country attend. With great enthusiasm, a member of the church missions committee introduces the family to the international students, saying, "We would like to introduce you to our missionaries to your country." Needless to say the family was not happy!
- A worker in a Muslim country is speaking at a church in the West about what God is doing in the Muslim world. He is not aware that a high-level official from a Muslim country is in the audience.
- Missionaries were recently imprisoned for a support email that was intercepted by the government of the country where they live. They were charged with sedition because of a sarcastic political comment in this private email to supporters.
- Bonnie Witherall was gunned down in Lebanon. She was a nurse serving with Operation Mobilization as a relief and development worker. A few hours after her martyrdom, a journalist called the leader of her team and asked if Bonnie was engaged in proselytism. He said, "No,

Part I: Introduction

she wasn't. She was doing relief and development." The journalist replied, "That's not what your website says about your work!"

CAUGHT IN THE CLASH OF PARADIGMS: VIEWING LIFE IN "3D"

The good news is that the global interconnectedness of communication has many positive repercussions. But it also requires those who are spokespersons for ministry to think carefully about the way they communicate. Paul's exhortations to the Colossians prove relevant in the Internet age:

"Be wise in the way you act toward outsiders; make the most of every opportunity. Let your conversation be always full of grace, seasoned with salt, so that you may know how to answer everyone" (Col 4:5–6, NIV).

Paul calls us to walk in wisdom toward those who are "outsiders," that is, who are not followers of Jesus. He then describes the practical expression of wisdom in five ways. First, he urges us to make the most of the opportunities before us. This means we should assume outsiders are listening and should communicate accordingly. (Indeed, in Paul's day where gatherings mostly took place in homes, nonbelieving friends, family, or household members were listening and watching.) In a glocalized world, we have greater opportunities to bear witness to Jesus. It also means we have a greater possibility of miscommunicating.

Second, Paul urges us to communicate graciously (or winsomely). Always! Sadly, many Christian leaders have made statements about Muslims that have been far from gracious. Third, our communication should be "seasoned with salt"—creative and compelling. Fourth, "know how to answer everyone" indicates that we should tailor our communication to each person. In a glocalized world, that means we focus on the person or persons we are sharing with, while at the same time realizing that our message may go beyond them to multiple audiences.

Fifth, note the purpose of these exhortations. Paul assumes we are answering people's questions: "so that you know how to answer everyone." It assumes we are actually engaged in a level of friendship with outsiders, highlighting the give and take of real relationships.

I began feeling this challenge of communicating to multiple audiences in the 1990s when I served as US Director of Frontiers. I would travel around the US to recruit for our cause. On the flights to different cities and churches, I would work on my PowerPoint presentations. In the early days of my work, this was no problem. I didn't mind if people saw what I was working on. But as time went on, the ethnic and religious diversity of my fellow passengers changed. With increased pluralism there were more Hindus, Muslims, or Buddhists sitting beside me. My presentations focused on recruiting people to reach the "other" and the "other" was sitting next to me. I want to share my faith with everyone I can. But recruiting people to share their faith and sharing one's faith are two different things. My world was changing, and how I lived out my faith demanded change as well.

The interconnectedness of a glocal world means that we cannot communicate with each audience separately. What we say in any public setting can be heard or read around the world. In the past, we could tailor our message for a particular audience, but no longer. What is spoken to one audience is too often overheard by others.

As mentioned previously, I address this challenge through "three-dimensional (3D) communication." I will illustrate this with Christian-Muslim relations, but the concept transfers to our communication with any other religious group (and as I said earlier, it has relevance for non-Christians as well). Our communication is 3D because, whether we like it or not, we communicate to three audiences simultaneously: Christian, Muslim, and secular. At the very least, it is 2D: Christian and non-Christian.

How can we address the complexity of communicating with multiple audiences? In light of the cultural shifts in our world today, I propose that the church must reevaluate three core concepts: our message, our identity, and our mandate. We need to clarify a core message worth dying for, a core identity worthy living for, and a core dream worth suffering for. We need to view life in "3D": three global trends (terrorism, pluralism, and globalization), three audiences (Christian, Muslim, and secular), and three aspects of our lives (a message, an identity, and a mandate).

What I am saying here has relevance to individuals, but it is particularly important for churches and organizations. I write this book as a "recovering" evangelical missions leader. I have poured my life into the fulfillment of the Great Commission for the last thirty years. I plan on continuing to do so until the day I die. But *how* I approach the Great Commission now is radically different.

I am recovering because I have found the terminology, perspectives, and paradigms of evangelical missions to be well intentioned, but lacking. I am weary of an approach that no longer fits our context, one that hampers rather than facilitates. For many of us, the present missions industry

Part I: Introduction

feels like Saul's armor on a young David. To a generation of young Davids (both men and women) I say, "Take off Saul's armor and follow Jesus into a glocalized world! May you be a visionary generation like the tribe of Issachar, "who understood the times and knew what God's people should do" (1 Chron 12:32, author's translation)."

3

Paradigm Shifts and Heart Renewal

Jesus always—ALWAYS—puts the emphasis of his teaching on heart issues, not behavioral routines. If the heart is right, loving actions will follow.

Bruxy Cavey

A group of leaders were having a serious, lively discussion about the challenges of glocalization and the Great Commission. During a break, Bill and John continued the dialogue, which at this point had become a debate. They raised their voices as they argued back and forth about the need for new communicational strategies. Finally, Bill pointed his finger at John and concluded, "It's not enough that we change our wording; we need a change in our being!"

For the past thirty-five years the Great Commission has been my guiding force. Matthew 28:18–20 has always been my favorite version of Jesus' mandate. The actual commission entails four activities: go, make disciples, baptize, and teach. We make disciples by going, baptizing, and teaching. The word "all" dominates this mandate. All authority has been given to Jesus. All nations must be discipled. All the commands must be obeyed. And Jesus promised to be with his disciples, literally, "all" the days. This commission is great!

Part I: Introduction

I used to teach about the "four alls" of the Great Commission, but in reality one of the alls dominated the others. I was preoccupied with "all the nations." That was the goal of the Great Commission and the goal of my life. I knew the names and numbers of people groups that had no or little witness of Jesus in their language. I counted them and measured success in light of them. I led countless intercessory prayer groups for them. I joined causes, attended conferences, pursued graduate degrees, purchased journal subscriptions, and bought hundreds of books—all related to the Great Commission. I measured success by the number of groups we engaged, the number of people that we trained to live cross-culturally, the number of new initiatives we started. I clearly favored the quantitative dimension of the Great Commission over the qualitative dimension.

Some people and organizations are called to this quantitative approach. I bless them and love them. In fact, I have many good friends who specialize in the quantitative focus. But an overemphasis on the quantitative dimension of obedience to the Great Commission can have negative repercussions. At least it did for me.

My heart shriveled because I viewed people as projects and targeted them for "the cause." They were objects for my agenda. The beauty of Jesus and his command to love got lost in this lopsided approach to the Great Commission. When someone mentioned an unreached people group it was as if I saw a target on their head. They were not people to be loved, but tasks to be accomplished. Instead of *being* a witness I had to witness "at them." Biblically, I knew that God was the one who converts people, but in practice I acted as if the Great Commission meant that I was the great converter!

Now don't get me wrong. There is clearly a quantitative dimension to the Great Commission. But in my experience, some evangelicals are woefully out of balance. This emphasis can unwittingly undermine Jesus' commission.

One of the most profound and heart-wrenching examples of this took place in Rwanda. In the 1980s Rwanda was considered one of the greatest examples of evangelistic breakthrough in Africa. Over 85 percent of the country was "Christian." Thousands upon thousands "prayed to receive Christ." Multitudes were swept into the church. But apparently many of them were not swept into the kingdom.

Within a decade darkness descended, and Rwanda became a blood bath. An estimated 800,000 people were killed, often hacked to death with machetes by their neighbors and fellow church members. Churches became slaughterhouses instead of sanctuaries. Hutu "Christians" would actually take communion and then leave the church to butcher Tutsis. The vast majority of Christians in Rwanda faithfully attended church, but few followed the crucified Messiah. The blood of tribalism ran deeper than the waters of baptism. Because of this, "the most Christianized country in Africa became the site of its worst genocide."

Rwanda illustrates what happens when Jesus' witnesses only try to save souls—the Christian church becomes a mile wide and an inch deep. This reflects the fruit of an overemphasis on the quantitative dimension of the Great Commission. Jesus commissions us to make obedient disciples. He wants followers, not fans!

By the grace of God, numerous factors have been balancing my life focus. I now have a greater hunger for the qualitative dimension of the Great Commission. I enjoy a more robust, holistic understanding of the gospel and the church's mandate. I want to model the message, not just communicate it verbally; to demonstrate the kingdom, not just talk about it.

I remain burdened for all nations (because Jesus is!) but I realize this must be the whole church's concern, not just mine. There are great leaders, organizations, and networks that have made this their goal. Yes, I still suffer from a messiah complex, and I sometimes feel like the salvation of the world rests upon my shoulders, but I am being healed. So the Lord has me pioneering new areas and growing in new ways.

HOW THE WHOLE GOSPEL MAKES US WHOLE

I was raised in Southern California, where I surfed, played football, and grew up with mountain lions, monkeys, and honey bears. I embraced the "sex, drugs, and rock and roll" lifestyle of the sixties. Then in 1970 I encountered Jesus, and my life radically changed. I experienced God's love and forgiveness through what is now known as the "Jesus Movement." I became a zealous "Jesus Freak," eager to change the world. My fellow zealots and I stayed busy handing out tracts and witnessing on the streets. You would often see us extending our index finger in the air signaling that there is only one way to heaven: Jesus!

I grew up with a partial understanding of the gospel, what I call the "gospel of evacuation." Jesus' death and resurrection was all about getting to heaven when you die. This kind of gospel, which is taught in certain

Part I: Introduction

evangelical churches, focuses primarily on the last few chapters of each of the four Gospels. The gospel of evacuation stresses Jesus' death, resurrection, and his Great Commission. It focuses on a personal relationship with Christ and on getting to heaven.

A few years ago, I was talking about Peace Catalyst International at a meeting, when a woman exclaimed, "But if people don't come to Christ, everything else is worthless!" Worthless? Really? Jesus said that our good deeds, such as peacemaking, glorify our Father in heaven (Matt 5:16). That sounds important. But the gospel of evacuation somehow misses that.

I rejoice in the blessings of my spiritual heritage. But in some ways, it resembles the gospel preached in Rwanda. It focuses too little on life on earth—except to get other people to heaven. It practically ignores Jesus' teaching and example —which makes up *most* of the content of the four Gospels!

Jesus *is* the gospel—not just his death and resurrection—but also his person, birth,3 example, and teaching. When I look at this Jesus, I realize that he taught and embodied the "*gospel of transformation.*" This gospel is not just about Jesus and "my personal salvation." He came to reconcile "all things"—restoring and healing individuals and *all* creation (Col 1:20). This good news describes the in-breaking of the kingdom of God, impacting all of life. The gospel of transformation is not just about getting to heaven (although that's part of it) but about bringing heaven to earth! That's what Jesus means when he teaches us to pray in the Lord's Prayer: "Your kingdom come. Your will be done, *on earth* as it is in heaven" (Matthew 6:10, emphasis mine). In other words, Jesus came to usher in a resistance movement known as the kingdom of God. This kingdom focuses on our relationship with God *and* neighbor, with personal purity *and* social justice, with reconciled relationships *and* creation care.

Here is how this grasp of the gospel of transformation impacted me. When I started on my journey with Jesus I focused on the Great Commission. I became part of a community that proudly described themselves as "*Great Commission Christians.*" We took Jesus' command to make disciples of all nations seriously. I still do!

But over the years, I came to realize there was more to following Jesus than the Great Commission. For example, what do we do with our friends and acquaintances if they don't respond to Christ? We love them! The Great Commandments—wholehearted love for God and love of neighbor—have become increasingly important to me. So I am no longer just a

Great Commission Christian, I am also a *"Great Commandment Christian."* Whether my neighbors respond to the gospel or not I must love them. I knew this theoretically in the past, but I have a profound experiential realization that the Great Commandment truly governs the Great Commission.

Finally, I am also a *"Sermon on the Mount Christian."* I take Jesus' teaching in Matthew 5–7 and Luke 6:20–49 seriously. This means I am called to be a peacemaker and to love my enemy. Note the clear link between these tasks:

"Blessed are the peacemakers, for they will be called *children of God*" (Matt 5:9).

"But I say to you, love your enemies and pray for those who persecute you, so that you may be *children of your Father in heaven*" (Matt 5:44–45).

What do God's children do? They make peace, and they love their enemies!

Embracing this gospel of transformation changes our heart, increases our joy, and makes us more whole.

FROM GLOBAL VISION TO INWARD JOURNEY

During the end of my tenure as international director of Frontiers, my wife Fran shared some things she had learned on a spiritual retreat in Ireland. We both chuckled when she told the story of one man's mission statement. He said, "My mission is to know that I am God's beloved child." Why did we laugh? You see, we were "Great Commission Christians." We understood what the *real* mission was. We didn't consider this man's pursuit worthy to be called a mission statement.

We no longer laugh about that mission statement. In fact, we think it's beautiful. Incomplete, but beautiful. Why the change of heart? Because these "Great Commission Christians" have encountered the contemplative prayer tradition. God has been leading us into an inward journey. In fact, Fran has become a full-time spiritual director, helping people on their inward journey of spiritual formation. She helps me a lot too!

Contemplative practice and spiritual formation are part of the gospel of transformation. I need heart renewal so I can follow Jesus with greater integrity. I need this inward journey so I can manifest Jesus more powerfully.

I am happy to say that mainstream evangelical institutions embrace the importance of the inward journey of spiritual formation:

- Westmont College, my alma mater, has a program in spiritual formation.
- Biola University and the Talbot School of Theology offers a master's program in Spiritual Formation and Soul Care.
- Denver Seminary, where I presently lecture, offers a Master of Divinity in Spiritual Formation.
- Fuller Seminary, my alma mater, offers a Doctor of Ministry in Spiritual Formation.

Ignatius of Loyola—the founder of the Jesuits—has had a profound impact on my inward journey. Ignatius was a Great Commission Christian with a contemplative bent. He embraced both a global vision and an inward journey.

I love his prayer model, *examen*, where you learn how to discern what God is doing in your life through a combination of gratitude, rational reflection on the events of the day, and attention to your feelings. The *examen* prayer grounds me in what is happening to me right now, right here. It helps me see where God is working and discern what God is saying. Awareness of my thoughts and feelings, while at times uncomfortable, allows God to show me the motives that really drive the things I do. This simple prayer of awareness and openness to hear God helps me be much more attentive to the still, small voice of the Good Shepherd throughout the day.

So what's the point I am trying to make by sharing with you about my inward journey? Our busy lifestyles and evangelical methodologies often hinder the very thing God wants to do in us. God is deeply concerned about pure motives, loving relationships, and inner freedom. The contemplative prayer tradition has helped me to grow in these three areas. Through the contemplative prayer tradition, I have also realized that my feelings or emotions—and not just my mind—are important in discerning God's voice.

I think we evangelicals have a lot of "heart work" to do.

FROM CONVERSION OF OTHERS TO CONVERSION OF SELF

Understanding the gospel of transformation and the practice of contemplative prayer has increased my joy and deepened my peace. It has also led to greater humility. I cringe when I realize how triumphalist I used to be, thinking in terms of "winning"—winning converts, churches, hearts, donors . . . you name it. I think winning someone to Christ, can be used in the positive sense of being winsome (1 Cor 9:19–23). But I had gone beyond winsomeness to competitiveness.

We rejoice when a "soul is saved," and cry and get angry when these very souls are persecuted by "the enemy." But do we stop to think that maybe these "enemies" are hurting, reeling, and confused as to why their family member betrayed them to follow Jesus? Who hurts for them? We depict them as monsters, but are they really? And what about the practice of missionary newsletter writing and mission-Sunday sermons in which we divulge personal information about the people we work with? We tell their stories rather carelessly, needing our supporters and fellow Christians to think more highly of our noble efforts to save them.

We forget to protect the dignity of those we serve. Would we like it if the shoe were on the other foot? What if our lives were being discussed and prayed over because someone we trusted talked about us? I still fervently believe that Jesus is the way, the truth, and the life (John 14:6). He *is* the way, and his way *is* the way of humility (Matt 5:3, 11:29; Phil 2:3–8). As his follower, I am called to imitate that humility.

I love the growth in humility modeled in the life of Paul the apostle. In his early letters he sees himself as the "least of the apostles" (1 Cor 15:9). As he matured he described himself as "very least of all the saints" (Ephesians 3:8). Finally, in his last days, he viewed himself as "chief of sinners" (1 Tim 1:15, KJV). What a beautiful downward trajectory of humility. The New International Version reads like this: "Here is a trustworthy saying that deserves full acceptance: Christ Jesus came into the world to save sinners—of whom I am the worst" (1 Tim 1:15).

This is how I like to describe our global mandate now. Jesus came into the world to save sinners. That is the good news. That is a confession deserving wholehearted acceptance. We can stake our life on it . . . and I have! But please note Paul's addition to this confession. "I am the worst" [of sinners]. Paul described his sinfulness in the present tense—"I am"—and he understood his Greek tenses better than anyone reading this book!

Apparently Paul had gone on the inward journey and knew the breadth and depth of evil lurking in his heart. This confession brought him joy because Jesus came to save sinners like him. This confession kept him humble because he knew the darkness residing within, especially as he walked with "the King of kings and Lord of lords . . .who lives in unapproachable light" (1 Tim 6:15–16).

Here's what this means for me. In the past I focused on converting others. Now I am much more concerned about my own ongoing conversion, and that frees me up to love more fully.

As a Sermon on the Mount Christian, I put a much greater emphasis on getting the log out of my own eye before worrying about others (Matt 7:3–5). Carl Medearis sums up this orientation well in one of his blog posts. He argues that the truism "love the sinner, hate the sin" is wrong. He concludes: "Hate my sin. Love sinners. It's my new motto."

Here's how I try to apply this in practice. When individuals want to join my organization, Peace Catalyst International (PCI), we ask them about why they want to join a peacemaking organization. People who want to join PCI are typically people who love Muslims and who want to reach out to them. Because of this, we are serious about helping them determine if PCI fits, or if what they really want is a mission agency.

We do not do peacemaking as an evangelistic strategy in PCI. We do it because that is what God's children do (Matt 5:9), because it glorifies God (Matt 5:16), and because we are commanded to (Rom 12:18; Heb 12:14). We don't want people joining PCI with a bait-and-switch approach to Muslims. Sure, we hope to share our faith as any true follower of Jesus would. But we are serious about pure motives and our peacemaking mandate.

I want to spend the rest of my life figuring out how the Sermon on the Mount and the Great Commandment guide me in peacemaking and make me more faithful to Jesus and winsome in my witness.

FROM MILITARY METAPHORS TO GOSPEL LANGUAGE

Perhaps the triumphalist or unloving aspects of our approach to missions can best be seen in the language that we use. Modern missions have tended to focus on military metaphors and triumphal slogans to describe the church's global mandate. And I was the chief of sinners.

When I was a young leader I loved military metaphors. I described an important aspect of my philosophy of ministry as "militancy." I saw myself more as a general in the military than I did as an ambassador of Christ. We were soldiers in a battle, on a rescue mission for God. I would often preach sermons on Joshua and Caleb "taking the land" as an illustration of the Great Commission today. It is true that Joshua and Caleb displayed amazing faith and bold obedience to God in their military exploits. Their example still stirs my heart and makes me want to emulate their faith and obedience. But I no longer see that story as a good illustration of what it means to fulfill the Great Commission.

I vividly remember a breakthrough moment I had regarding how we communicate about missions. I was attending the Consultation on Mission Language and Metaphors at Fuller Theological Seminary in June 1–3, 2000. We had spent almost two days wrestling with commonly used terms and metaphors to describe our calling. Paul Pierson, professor of history at the Fuller School of Intercultural Studies, interrupted the discussion: "Why don't we use the Abrahamic mandate to bless all nations to describe what we do?" I felt God's peace. In the depths of my heart I sensed this felt right. Here was a biblical term that described our calling in a much more relevant and relational way than the terms presently used. I trashed my old sermon notes on Joshua and Caleb.

Military metaphors and triumphal slogans not only miscommunicate, but they also shape the way we view the people we are supposed to love. Does our warfare imagery subconsciously lead us to perceive unreached people groups as the "enemy"? A horrendous example of this misuse of the metaphor is available on the website of a leading seminary. A video clip portrays the evangelization of their neighborhoods as a military operation with actual footage of people with guns! Imagine how the people living in the neighborhoods around the seminary might feel if they saw this video.

Here's another illustration. One of the emerging elders of the church in a North African country, a Muslim-background believer, was surfing the Internet. He found a Christian website that spoke about the great things God was doing in his country. This ministry boasted of establishing "beachheads" and believed the gospel would go forth with power. Soon the country would be conquered for Christ. From his perspective, this group was planning a literal military invasion of his country. He understood this as holy war! If a mature and educated Muslim-background believer perceives these military metaphors as literal truths, how much more the average Muslim?

Even if he had not interpreted this invasion as being literal, this kind of language would have made him feel like he and his countrymen were perceived as enemies to be conquered or objects of colonization—not exactly how Jesus wants us to view fellow human beings.

Part I: Introduction

I see at least two major reasons for military metaphors in the New Testament. The first is for the sake of comparison. There are significant parallels between the Christian life and the life of a soldier. Just as a soldier must be disciplined, must suffer, and must display singleness of purpose, so too must the Christian (2 Tim 2:3–4).

The second is for the sake of contrast. These metaphors are used primarily to contrast Christians' spiritual warfare with literal warfare. Our real enemy is the devil. As Paul says, "For our struggle is not against enemies of blood and flesh, but against . . . the spiritual forces of evil in the heavenly places" (Eph 6:12). "For though we walk in the flesh, we do not war according to the flesh" (2 Cor 10:3, NASB).

In contrast to evangelical literature and strategy, the New Testament does not use military metaphors to describe the task of evangelism. Evangelism in the New Testament is not portrayed in military terms. Paul does not put on "crusades," "mobilize," "establish beachheads," or "target" a people. In other words, evangelicals have extended the meaning of military metaphors beyond the intent of New Testament authors.

As I will argue in the rest of the book, terrorism, pluralism, and globalization force us to consider more appropriate metaphors for ministry in the third millennium. Like the biblical authors, we must contextualize our metaphors for maximum impact with minimum distortion. Therefore, it would be prudent and contextually sensitive to find and use more nonmilitary metaphors. Instead of military metaphors, we can use gospel language like "blessing" (Gen 12:1–3; Gal 3:8), "peacemaking" (Matt 5:9; Eph 2:11–17; Col 1:20; Rom 14:19), or "the ministry of reconciliation" (2 Cor 5:18–19).

Jesus said, "out of the abundance of the heart the mouth speaks" (Matt 12:34), highlighting the vital connection between our heart and our words. According to Jesus, our words merely reflect what's in our heart. So I have to conclude that this overemphasis on military metaphors says something about our hearts.

This book is very much about communication. I am arguing that we need to change our wording. But we need a change in our *being* as well. The global paradigm shifts that we face today invite personal heart renewal. May we all hear afresh the voice of the Good Shepherd who longs to restore our souls and lead us into paths of righteousness for his name's sake (Ps 23:3).

PART II

A Core Message Worth Dying For

4

Jesus-Centered

> Jesus is the gospel—he himself is the good news.
>
> E. STANLEY JONES

My friend Carl Medearis tells an enlightening story about teaching at a large church in Texas. He asked the group, "what is the gospel?" and then made a list of the students' answers on the chalkboard. They answered, "the free gift of God, freedom from sin, eternal life, grace, unconditional love, healing and deliverance, redemption, faith in God, new life."

Next he asked the class if they missed anything. The class sat silent for a minute. Then a girl raised her hand and asked, "How come none of us mentioned Jesus?"

Notice that everything listed on the chalkboard was true. They described important aspects of the gospel. But check out the focus on theological propositions. Somehow the person, Jesus, got pushed to the fringes—almost left out. I think this reflects a tendency in many evangelical churches. I know this has been true of me.

A JESUS-CENTERED CORE MESSAGE

A core message is what we freely share with anyone, anywhere, all the time. Click on any website and you will find a core message. The better the website

Part II: A Core Message Worth Dying For

and wiser the organization, the clearer the core message. The core message (whether slogan, vision, or mission statement) is what we convey publically to the world—to all three of our audiences: to people who have not heard of Jesus (of whatever faith), to an onlooking secular world, and to the church.

The core messages of different organizations and individuals may vary, but the core message for the church is clear:

- "For I decided to know nothing among you except Jesus Christ, and him crucified" (1 Cor 2:2).
- "For I handed on to you as *of first importance* what I in turn had received: that Christ died for our sins in accordance with the scriptures, and that he was buried, and that he was raised on the third day in accordance with the scriptures" (1 Cor 15:3–4, emphasis mine).
- "He [Jesus] is the head of the body, the church; he is the beginning, the firstborn from the dead, so that he might come to have *first place in everything*" (Col 1:18, emphasis mine).

Jesus is the final revelation of God to humanity. God reveals himself to us in Jesus (John 1:18). If someone wants to know what God is like, she needs to look at Jesus. Anyone who has seen Jesus has seen God (John 14:9; Heb 1:1–3).

Jesus himself teaches that he is the central message, the focal point of the Scriptures that we refer to as the Old Testament (John 5:39; Luke 24:25–27).

So Jesus Himself is Jesus-centered! He emphatically and repeatedly teaches that he is at the center of the kingdom of God. He is the fulfillment of Old Testament promises and the source of eternal life. Entrance to the kingdom depends on how people respond to him.

Jesus is our example, teacher, friend, savior, and Lord. And so we center our lives on him and the good news about him. When we remain focused on Jesus, he transforms us. Ultimately this core message changes the core of our being.

Jesus is our core message—Jesus, not the religion of Christianity, not Western civilization, and not "God bless America" patriotism. Jesus is the way, not Christianity. The famous evangelist to India in the twentieth century, E. Stanley Jones, described this well:

> When I go to India I have to apologize for many things—for Western civilization, for it is only partly Christianised; for the Christian

Church, for it too is only partly Christianised; for myself, for I am only a Christian-in-the-making; but when it comes to Jesus, there are no apologies on my lips, for there are none in my heart. He is our one perfect possession.[1]

So what's the big deal about being Jesus-centered? As I have demonstrated above, Jesus is the center of the Bible and thus our core message. But we also need to be radically Jesus-centered for the sake of effective communication. My friend Carl Medearis wisely notes: "Jesus doesn't come loaded with bias, prejudice, conflict or war. Christianity often does."[2]

So we need to make a clear distinction between "cultural Christianity" and Jesus. People are impressed with Jesus but often depressed about the church or Christianity. Too many people confuse Christendom with Christ. And this confusion makes all the difference in the world . . . and in the world to come!

The "conversion" of the emperor Constantine in the fourth century marks the birth of cultural Christianity. Positively "God used Constantine to end a sometimes bloody persecution and to, among other things, call together the church to put down a deadly heresy or two."[3] But overall his conversion was a negative turning point in the history of the church. In the first three centuries, prior to Constantine, the church lived as a persecuted minority. Persecuted but powerful, the church had a massive impact on the Roman Empire.

The conversion experience of Constantine radically impacted the meaning of the gospel and the history of Christianity. On the eve of a battle on the outskirts of Rome, Constantine reportedly saw the sign of the cross in the sky with the words beneath that cross: under this sign conquer. He took that as an omen and painted the sign of Christ crucified on his weapons of war. The next day Constantine won a decisive victory.

Henceforth, the cross came to symbolize imperial power. It stood for military might rather than sacrificial love. Instead of the willingness to die for their faith, Constantinian Christians became focused on killing for their faith. "Taking up the cross" meant readiness to kill rather than dying to self. Under Constantine, the church and state became one. Christians possessed political power. Christian theocracy was birthed, meaning that state violence was both sanctioned and "sanctified"!

1. Roberts Jr., *Glocalization*, 155.
2. Medearis, *Muslims, Christians, and Jesus*, 51.
3. Moore, *Onward*, 34.

Part II: A Core Message Worth Dying For

Under Constantine, the once dynamic movement called the church became institutionalized.

Whereas it once was incarnational (or missional), it now became attractional. The focus was on people attending a fancy cathedral on Sunday rather than incarnating the gospel in the workplace from Monday through Saturday. The church became associated with sacred buildings, sacraments, and professional clergy.

The result? Christendom led to the creation and development of Western civilization (wrongly perceived as "Christian" culture). Up until the modern era, the world was divided into "Christendom" and "heathendom" (similar to how Muslims divided up the world into *Dar al-Islam*, the house of Islam, and *Dar al-Harb*, the house of war). In certain eras of Christendom, there was no freedom of religion. In fact, it imposed its faith and morality on everyone (this is what theocracies do—sounds a lot like Saudi Arabia or Iran doesn't it?).

In spite of this, there have been reform movements throughout the history of the church. Powerful and positive things have been done by Jesus through an imperfect church. The church has faithfully witnessed to the ends of the earth. And Jesus' people have been a major force in promoting education and health care around the world, abolishing slavery, doing relief and development, and promoting human rights.

But . . . there still remains a huge difference between Christendom and Christ. I agree with Stuart Murray:

> The Christendom era has bequeathed a form of Christianity that has marginalized, spiritualized, domesticated, and emasculated Jesus. The teaching of Jesus is watered down, privatized, and explained away. Jesus is worshipped as a remote kingly figure or a romanticized personal savior. In many churches (especially those emerging from the Reformation), Paul's writings are prioritized over the Gospel accounts of the life of Jesus.[4]

Our religious and secular friends may be allergic to Christianity, but most find Jesus attractive. Many of them respect true followers of Jesus.

The good news about Jesus is our core message.

One of the greatest ways to discern the core message of your life is to answer this question: what message am I willing to die for?

I would rather not die for American foreign policy. Frankly, I am not willing to die for the religion of Christianity. But by the grace of God, I

---

4. Murray, *The Naked Anabaptist*, 55.

would be willing to die for Christ and for the right of everyone to know of Christ's love.

Jesus said, "If any want to become my followers, let them deny themselves and take up their cross daily and follow me" (Luke 9:23, NRS). Since the cross was an instrument of death, Jesus meant that we must be willing to die to ourselves and be willing to die for him.

Glocalization means that we can no longer have a different message or be a different person for each different audience. In the core of our being, we have to have the same message and personal identity for every audience. This doesn't mean everyone will necessarily like the message, but we must eliminate deception or any perception of deception. We have a core message worth dying for if we can share that message freely with Christians, those of other religions, and the secular world, and if we wouldn't mind having that message on our websites (which will be read by all three audiences).

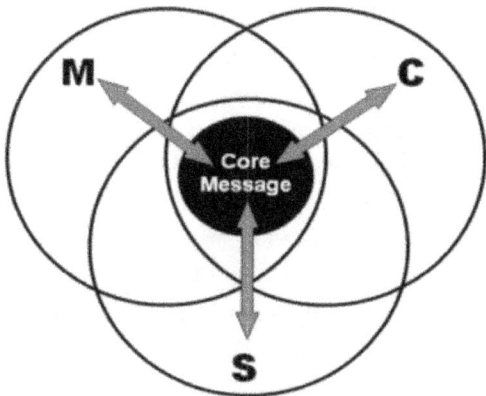

Figure 1.
3D Communication: Core Message

Figure 1 illustrates what I call three-dimensional (3D) communication. This illustration relates to Christian-Muslim relations, but the concept transfers to our communication with any other religious group. Our communication is 3D because we communicate to three audiences simultaneously. We seek to express our core message in a way that the church (represented in the diagram by the letter "C"), the Muslim world (represented by the letter "M"), and the secular world (represented by the letter "S") can all understand.

Part II: A Core Message Worth Dying For

The 3D model of communication emphasizes a core message that is communicated to all audiences. (In Figure 1, this is illustrated in the center, where the circles overlap.) At the same time, it acknowledges that we communicate contextualized applications of our core message to each audience (illustrated by the individual circles). Of course, our contextualized messages to each audience must connect clearly to our core message. (The arrow in the diagram extends from the core message to the three other audiences.)

Our public message—what we say anywhere to anyone—is our core message. This is what we say from our pulpits, on our websites, and in our emails. Our contextualized message is what we say in more private settings, as Jesus did with his disciples. But let me be clear about this. I am not proposing a more sophisticated approach to covering up our intentions. I am explaining a more nuanced approach to communication. Our contextualized message must be clearly rooted in our core message. Thus, if a noble-minded outsider heard us share both our core message and our contextualized message, she wouldn't accuse us of duplicity or lack of integrity. It would make sense to her.

While it is difficult to communicate a core message to three audiences simultaneously, it is not impossible. More to the point, it is necessary in the twenty-first century. A few years ago I spoke at a church about what God is doing in the Muslim world. Doing my best to communicate in a way that would be sensitive to a secular or Muslim audience, I explained that many Muslims are now following Jesus, and I challenged the church to love Muslims. After I spoke, a Muslim (not a Muslim-background believer—a Muslim) who happened to be visiting the church came up to me and said, "Thank you so much for your word this morning. This message needs to be heard throughout the United States!"

Understanding 3D communication equips us to walk in wisdom. We walk in wisdom when we realize that, especially in public settings (speaking at a church, writing articles or books, or posting something on the Internet), others will hear our message. Thus, we seek to craft our public messages so that they are relevant and sensitive to the three audiences.

Jesus-Centered

JESUS, CHURCH PLANTING, GOSPEL PLANTING, AND DISCIPLE-MAKING MOVEMENTS

So how does this focus on being radically Jesus centered relate to people and organizations who long to fulfill the Great Commission?

When I was international director of Frontiers, the focus of many missions organizations was church planting. I agree with the intent of the term (facilitating the creation of communities of Jesus' followers), but I believe that the term itself is inaccurate and unhelpful. I think what we really do is plant the gospel.

Although the New Testament contains many references to church and churches, nowhere does the New Testament imply that we plant the church. But it does teach that we plant the gospel. The parable of the sower makes this clear (Matt 13).

Gospel planting helps us envision our task more clearly. The term *church planting* implies that we bring the church from the outside. To use another metaphor, church planting implies that we plant the gospel seed along with a "western" flowerpot. The church is then foreign rather than indigenous. Gospel planting implies that we sow the gospel seed, allowing churches or communities of obedient Jesus followers to form indigenously in natural and organic ways of gathering.

Gospel planting is more Christ-centered than church planting, since Jesus is the gospel.

To hear a critique of church planting can be difficult for most organizations who build their strategy around this task. But this critique is necessary, first of all, for the sake of effective communication. The term *church* carries far too much unhelpful baggage in countries that we perceive as resistant to the gospel. It focuses on buildings and programs, rather than people. It conjures up images of the West and the past (colonialism) that hinder what God wants to do in the present. Thus, in most cases I prefer functional definitions of the term *church*. Communities of Jesus' followers, Christ-centered communities, or core groups who follow Jesus are the preferred options most of the time.

Second, this critique is necessary for biblical reasons. Paul's apostolic self-description indicates that his goal was the gospel. Yes, his work resulted in communities of Jesus' followers. Yes, he loved and suffered for these communities of faith. But he linked his apostolic aims and ambitions with the gospel.

I like the more recent emphasis on Disciple-Making Movements (DMM). This term is more biblically accurate than church planting (Matt 28:19; Acts 14:21–23), and it is more Jesus-centered since a disciple by definition refers to one who "follows Jesus."

THE CORE MESSAGE AND THE CONTEXTUAL MESSAGE

When I speak to Christians, I emphasize different things than I do when I speak to Muslims or a secular audience. I contextualize or adapt my message to my audience. By adapting to one audience, I build my message on shared assumptions and may use technical terms that most outsiders don't understand. This allows me to communicate more deeply and effectively.

I may also want to share about important issues privately—in a more heart-to-heart fashion. Organizations of all types need to set apart times for sharing confidential personal and strategic information.

But when I speak to only one audience, I always remember two things. First, what would the other audiences think if they heard me say these things? When I speak to Christians I try to imagine some of my Muslim and secular friends sitting in the audience. This helps me communicate with greater wisdom, grace, and integrity. Second, I ask myself: does this contextual message connect with my core message? Am I being consistent? Depending on which audience I address, as I speak I think: would my Muslim, Christian, or secular friends understand this as being congruent with my core message?

5

Jesus-Centered and Kingdom-Focused

> We need a holistic gospel because the world is in a holistic mess!
>
> CHRISTOPHER J. H. WRIGHT

James Choung's *True Story: A Christianity Worth Believing In* tells a captivating story about a Christian named Caleb struggling with his faith on a college campus. Caleb grew up believing the gospel of evacuation. His faith was primarily about a personal relationship with Christ and getting to heaven. When confronted about things like injustice, poverty, and environmental devastation by Anna, a girl he was attracted to, Caleb's faith seemed irrelevant. He asks, "Is everything besides going to heaven extra credit?"

Over time, Caleb comes to realize that the gospel is all about Jesus, and it is about all of life. The gospel is not just about the afterlife, but also about embodying Christ in this life. Caleb's journey to understanding the big story of the gospel parallels my journey in many ways.

This chapter will be pretty theological. So grab a cup of coffee, tea, or whatever your favorite beverage is, and sit down awhile as we look at two windows into a Jesus-centered, kingdom-focused gospel.

Part II: A Core Message Worth Dying For

THE FIRST WINDOW: JESUS CAME TO REVERSE THE CURSE!

Virtually everyone—Christian, atheist, animist, or nonreligious—agrees on one theological doctrine: the world is a mess. Theologians call this the doctrine of sin or "the fall." Newspapers call it headlines. I love how the well-known biblical scholar Chris Wright describes it: "We need a holistic gospel because the world is in a holistic mess!"[1]

Why are we in this holistic mess? The story of Adam and Eve's rebellion in Genesis 3 describes four big problems, or areas of alienation. First they (and all humanity) became alienated from God. Adam and Eve once enjoyed perfect fellowship with God. No barriers. Full intimacy, perfect delight. Because of sin, they hid from God. Instead of fellowship, they began to fear. The result? They were driven out of the garden of Eden. Sin results in *theological alienation*.

Second, they became alienated from one another. Adam and Eve were once naked and not ashamed (Gen 2:25). They enjoyed full transparency with one another. But because of sin, they began to feel shame. They made fig-leaf, designer clothes to cover up. Originally Adam and Eve were created in God's image as equal partners, blessed to rule the earth (Gen 1:26–28). But because of sin, Adam began to rule over Eve. Sin results in *sociological alienation*.

Implicit in their covering up is a third type of alienation. Sin fragmented their very personalities. They were once "true faced"; they became "two faced." Ever since the fall we find all kinds of masks to hide our shame and to portray ourselves differently than we feel inside. Sin results in *psychological alienation*.

Fourth, sin impacted humanity's relationship with the physical world. The earth is under a curse. Work is hard. Floods, famines, and fire wreak havoc. We are alienated from creation. Sin results in *ecological alienation*.

Thus, the impact of sin is multidimensional. It affects our relationship with God, our relationship with ourselves, our relationships with one another, and our relationship with creation. We are in a holistic mess.

So how does Jesus address this mess? Every evangelical would say that the gospel addresses our theological alienation. Through Jesus we get right with God; we are saved. So far so good. But this partial gospel doesn't address our holistic mess!

---

1. Wright, *The Mission of God*, 315.

Jesus-Centered and Kingdom-Focused

Jesus came to reverse the curse. *The results of sin are multidimensional. Thus, reconciliation is multidimensional.* The life, teaching, death, and resurrection of Christ address all four alienations of the fall.

As evangelicals we rightly love and preach the gospel of grace. But we often forget that the gospel is also called the gospel of peace. Because of this, the traditional evangelical proclamation of the gospel has often lacked social impact. Yet the two descriptions of the gospel are side by side in Ephesians. In the first section of Ephesians 2 (verses 1–10), Paul articulates his famous description of the gospel of grace. In the second section of Ephesians 2 (verses 11–22, and especially 13–17), he portrays the good news as the gospel of peace.

> But now in Christ Jesus you who once were far off have been brought near by the blood of Christ. For he is our peace; in his flesh he has made both groups into one and has broken down the dividing wall, that is, the hostility between us. He has abolished the law with its commandments and ordinances, that he might create in himself one new humanity in place of the two, thus making peace, and might reconcile both groups to God in one body through the cross, thus putting to death that hostility through it. So he came and proclaimed peace to you who were far off and peace to those who were near (Eph 2:13–17).

One can hardly overemphasize how radical this message of peace must have sounded to Paul's original audience. The relationship between Gentile and Jew could be described as a prototype of all division or racial alienation in the first century—comparable to the relationship between whites and blacks in the United States during the civil rights movement or in South Africa under apartheid. The animosity felt between many Americans and Muslims since 9/11 serves as a more up-to-date example.

Paul tells us that Christ's death has reconciled both Gentile and Jew to God (verse 16). Prior to Christ, Gentiles endured a double alienation. They were "without Christ . . . and without God in the world" and "aliens from the commonwealth of Israel" (Eph 2:12). But now, through Christ's death, they have experienced a double reconciliation—they have been reconciled to God and to one another. According to Paul, Jesus is our peace. Jesus makes peace. Jesus proclaims peace!

Through the gospel, the church becomes an alternative society, a community where humanity's divisions have been overcome. A foretaste of heaven's harmony. Anything less is a denial of the gospel and nature of the church.

So why is Sunday morning considered to be one of the most segregated times of the week? Why don't most churches model an alternative society reflecting heaven's harmony? Because far too many churches in the world teach and model the gospel of evacuation rather than the gospel of transformation. Or as Russell Moore says, they are not preaching the gospel but an "almost gospel."[2]

A second passage describing multidimensional reconciliation is Galatians 3:26–28:

> For in Christ Jesus you are all children of God through faith. As many of you as were baptized into Christ have clothed yourselves with Christ. There is no longer Jew or Greek, there is no longer slave or free, there is no longer male and female; for all of you are one in Christ Jesus.

The literary context of this passage ("As many of you as were baptized into Christ" in verse 27) implies that it was part of a baptismal formula, which underscores its significance. Imagine how profound baptism would be if the church reflected the socially explosive implications of the gospel. In South Africa, during apartheid, some churches made this important connection. During their baptism ceremonies, one Vineyard church publicly confessed: "I am no longer black or white, rich or poor, male nor female. I am now one in Jesus Christ and his people."

The cultural context gives us further insight into the radical nature of the gospel. A prayer Paul offered up every day as a Jew shows that the gospel countered the prevailing prejudice and demeaning attitude of society: "Blessed are you O Lord God, for you have not made me a Greek, you have not made me a woman, and you have not made me a slave." Wow! It's hard to imagine praying such a racist, sexist, and elitist prayer.

The baptismal formula in Galatians 3:26–28 describes Christ's revolutionary, reconciling purposes as they relate to the three great divisions in ancient times: (1) race (Jew and Gentile), (2) class (slave and free), and (3) gender (male and female).

Now for the grand finale—Paul's most comprehensive summary of the gospel:

---

2. Moore, *Onward*, 32, 172, 216–18.

> For in him all the fullness of God was pleased to dwell, and through him God was pleased to reconcile to himself all things, whether on earth or in heaven, by making peace through the blood of his cross (Col 1:19–20).

Note the Jesus-centeredness of this passage. God's fullness dwells in Jesus and reconciliation takes place through Jesus. But the gospel is not just about my personal salvation. He reconciles "all things" to himself, including things in heaven and earth. The cosmic scope of Christ's reconciliation is breathtaking—restoring and healing all creation. If this isn't a holistic gospel, I don't know what is!

The gospel overcomes the fourfold alienation (noted in Genesis 3) by bringing peace with God, self, others, and creation. Through his life, death, and resurrection, Jesus came to reverse the curse.

As the famous Christmas song "Joy to the World" proclaims:

> No more let sins and sorrows grow,
> Nor thorns infest the ground;
> He comes to make His blessings flow
> Far as the curse is found.

Jesus' blessings flow through the gospel as far as the curse is found. And they will flow until the curse is reversed. As the Lamb who was slain, Jesus will one day return and make all things new. He will establish a new heavens and a new earth. At that time we will exclaim with John the apostle: "*no longer will there be any curse.* The throne of God and the Lamb will be in the city, and his servants will serve him" (Rev 22:3, NIV, emphasis mine).

Jesus came to reverse the curse. This is a core message worth dying for!

THE SECOND WINDOW: JESUS CAME TO BRING HEAVEN TO EARTH

I have the privilege of serving in a denomination that believes in a holistic gospel. The Vineyard Association of Churches builds its entire ministry on the theology and experience of the kingdom of God. You can't get more comprehensive than that, and I love it!

However, I haven't always believed in a holistic gospel, and much of my work is with evangelicals who lack this holistic perspective. Many suffer from a truncated, reductionist gospel—a narrow understanding of the good news that focuses only on the spiritual part of life, values evangelism over all else, and mainly wants to get people to heaven.

I believe in the spiritual part of life, and I value evangelism, as long as we understand evangelism as bearing witness to Jesus and not converting people to Christianity. As far as getting people to heaven . . . I believe having an eternal perspective is hugely important.

But the gospel that Jesus preached, the gospel of the kingdom, is so much bigger than this. Jesus' goal is not just to get people to heaven. His goal is also to bring heaven to earth!

As I said previously, Jesus calls us to pray: "Your kingdom come. Your will be done, *on earth* as it is in heaven" (Matt 6:10, emphasis mine). Jesus came to destroy the works of the devil (1 John 3:8). That's what Jesus models when he says, "But if it is by the Spirit of God that I cast out demons, then *the kingdom of God has come to you*" (Matt 12:28, emphasis mine). In other words, every time Jesus healed the sick, cast out demons, fed the hungry, stilled a storm, granted forgiveness, or embraced the marginalized, Satan's kingdom was being destroyed and God's kingdom was coming to earth.

Jesus' ministry was a foretaste of heaven. Our ministry should be the same. The manifestation of God's kingdom in the present is a "preview of coming attractions"—pointing to the beauty and reality of the future kingdom. Bringing heaven to earth is one of the best ways of getting people to heaven. It models the "show and tell" method of witnessing. We show people what heaven is like right now, on earth. Then we tell them that this is because of Jesus. Yes, we do this imperfectly and only partially. But, these present kingdom acts are true signs of the future that reflect the gospel and point people to Jesus.

How does this gospel of the kingdom differ from the gospel that is preached by many evangelicals? I think it differs in two ways. First, evangelicals are skilled at sharing about salvation in Christ. But they aren't as good at helping those who have received Christ actually live as new creatures in Christ. Evangelicals usually focus more on gaining *entrance* into the kingdom than they do living out the *ethics* of the kingdom.

The gospel of the kingdom is an announcement of the rule of God breaking into the world through Christ. This is the core message worth dying for. But the kingdom comes through both the message and through the life of the messenger. In other words, heaven invades earth when Christ's followers embody the inside-out ethics of the kingdom. The kingdom of

God is manifested when we reflect purity of heart, humility of mind, and peaceable relationships (Matt 5:5, 8, 9). This is beautiful orthodoxy.

In his book, *The Next Christians*, Gabe Lyons rightly describes a second evangelical blind spot:

> God's story is made up of four key parts: creation, fall, redemption, restoration. . . . The truncated Gospel that is often recounted is faithful to the fall and redemption pieces of the story, but largely ignores the creation and restoration components.[3]

Gabe is right. Evangelicals have been splendid at communicating about the fall and redemption. But Jesus did not come only to save souls. He came to heal and restore a broken world (creation and restoration). The gospel is not just about personal salvation. The gospel is about making us new creatures *and* about God building a new creation.

In Christ, the new creation has begun. And what is one of the most profound and practical ways we build the new creation? Through the ministry of reconciliation:

> Therefore, if anyone is in Christ, he is a new creation; the old has gone, the new has come! All this is from God, who reconciled us to himself through Christ and gave us the ministry of reconciliation: that God was reconciling the world to himself in Christ, not counting men's sins against them. And he has committed to us the message of reconciliation (2 Cor 5:17–19, NIV).

According to Paul, reconciliation is the core of God's mission, summarizing both the gospel and the goal of the gospel. Reconciliation is the ultimate value of the new creation. Anything we do to facilitate reconciliation within families, organizations, or communities helps build the new creation.

To ignore the creation and restoration components of the gospel minimizes the Bible's story with devastating repercussions for our lives. Without a gospel rooted in creation (Genesis) and moving towards the new creation (Revelation) we lose the "big picture" of the Bible's story and become unfaithful to Jesus.

In the beginning, God created us, blessed us, and commissioned us. As God's image bearers, our mandate was to rule the earth—to cultivate and care for the world (Gen 1:26–28; 2:15). This first commission has never changed or been rescinded. Because we are created in God's image, all

---

3. Lyons, *The Next Christians*, 53.

humanity is inherently creative. Everyone is wired to figure out better ways of doing things, to cultivate beauty, to develop technology, to be productive. Whether consciously or unconsciously, despite sin and brokenness, every human being fulfills this commission, at least in part.

But something has gone terribly wrong. Divorce, injustice, murder, rape, genocide, war, and ecological devastation litter the history of humankind. God's good creation has been spoiled by evil and groans for deliverance.

And through Christ, deliverance will come. Creation will be renewed. Through Christ, people are saved and restored to rule the earth in a way that reflects God's image (and thus his original purposes). This is the good news that Peter, Paul, and John shared: "But we are looking forward to the new heavens and new earth he has promised, a world filled with God's righteousness" (2 Pet 3:13, NLT).

"For all creation is waiting eagerly for that future day when God will reveal who his children really are. Against its will, all creation was subjected to God's curse. But with eager hope, the creation looks forward to the day when it will join God's children in glorious freedom from death and decay" (Rom 8:19–21, NLT).

"For you [Jesus] were slaughtered, and your blood has ransomed people for God from every tribe and language and people and nation. And you have caused them to become a Kingdom of priests for our God. And they will reign on the earth" (Rev 5:9–10, NLT).

One thing we have in common with everyone—we all live in a broken world. And if we realize that the gospel addresses all of creation, we will partner with non-Christians as well as Christians in our common drive toward fulfilling the first commission. A gospel that includes creation and restoration motivates us to serve shoulder to shoulder with others seeking the common good. We would more naturally "seek the peace of the city," as Jeremiah exhorts us (Jer 29:7). We would find it easy to "always seek to do good to one another and to all," as Paul says (1 Thess 5:15). Peacemaking and all sorts of good works take on a whole new meaning.

Gabe Lyons calls people engaged in ministry like this "restorers":

> Telling others about Jesus is important, but conversion isn't their only motive. Their mission is to infuse the world with beauty, grace, justice, and love. I call them restorers because they envision the world as it was meant to be and they work toward that vision. Restorers seek to mend earth's brokenness. They recognize that the

world will not be completely healed until Christ's return, but they believe that the process begins now as we partner with God.[4]

The gospel of the kingdom is concerned about both getting people to heaven and bringing heaven to earth—a core message worth dying for!

---

4. Ibid., 47.

PART III

A Core Identity Worth Living For

6

An Integrated Identity

> Moral integrity is essential... to Christian Mission in the public arena. Integrity means there is no dichotomy between our private and public "face"; between the sacred and the secular in our lives.
>
> CHRISTOPHER J. H. WRIGHT

Heather Mercer and Dayna Curry were imprisoned by the Taliban in Afghanistan in 2001 for proselytizing. After a high-profile, dramatic release, they told a television reporter that they were aid workers who had not been proselytizing. Immediately, media worldwide broadcast a prayer card that identified them as missionaries. To the secular and Muslim worlds, missionaries by definition proselytize, and the press does not recognize the distinction between positive witness (which is what Heather and Dayna did) versus coercive proselytism. Two worlds collided, and these courageous, devout workers were caught in the clash between old and new paradigms of ministry. They felt the pain of their dual identity being exposed in the public square.

Anyone involved in following Jesus among the nations—especially those who live in contexts that are hostile to the Christian faith—will face identity issues. This is also increasingly true of those who serve in some form of ministry among their neighbors in their countries of origin.

How do you explain yourself?

Part III: A Core Identity Worth Living For

In the process of writing this book, a friend of mine said this on Facebook: "Just hearing your thoughts on glocalization has helped us in our thinking through our true identity individually and as a community in New Orleans. I have found that once someone knows and becomes comfortable with their identity it makes it easier to build bridges and friendships in the community."

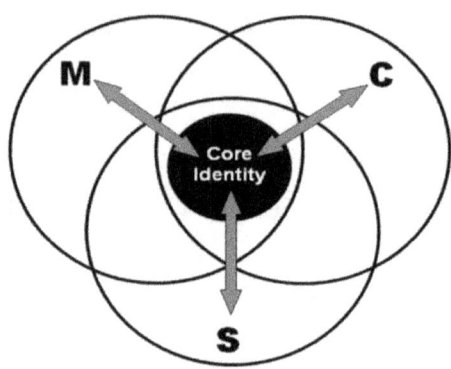

Figure 2.
3D Communication: Core Identity

Identity issues become even more difficult if you live in another country. How do you explain why you have moved from your home country?

In the past, many felt they could successfully maintain different identities in two worlds. To their Christian constituency (churches and supporters), they were known as missionaries. In their adopted homeland, they were businesspeople, educators, relief workers, or "tentmakers" of some other sort. But today's interconnected world has heightened the tension of maintaining this dual identity.

Such a dual identity results in low-grade anxiety for some, who feel as though they are hiding their true identity in order to share the truth about Christ. Nagging fears of appearing to be dishonest can muddle anyone's conscience, rob one's joy, and gradually erode boldness in sharing the gospel.

A dual identity reflects not only a split personality, but split spirituality—a false understanding that spiritual aspects of our life or our work are more important than the practical parts of life. In other words, one of the underlying reasons for split spirituality is the false and unbiblical dichotomy between the sacred and secular, the physical and spiritual. Most

An Integrated Identity

evangelicals would deny this theologically, but their heart and practice often model this bifurcated lifestyle. Many find it hard to internalize and practice the holistic demands of Scripture.

An international evangelical document called *The Cape Town Commitment* describes the secular-sacred divide as a major obstacle to fulfilling God's purposes and calls upon Christians everywhere to reject its unbiblical assumptions and resist its damaging effects. It challenges church leaders to understand the strategic impact of ministry in the workplace and to mobilize, equip, and send out their church members as witnesses into the workplace, both in their own local communities and around the world.

A core identity speaks of integrity and integration—words that come from the same Latin root: to make whole. Integrity refers to consistency between inner convictions and outward actions. We walk in integrity when we have "truth in the inward being" (Ps 51:6).

Having an integrated identity worth living for means that we have aligned our motivation, our work, our personal gifting, and our calling. In other words, moved by the love of Christ, we seek ways of living and serving that fit the way God has made us. This is what leadership guru Bobby Clinton calls "ministering out of being." This allows us to follow Jesus among the nations with integrity and boldness.

Paul the apostle models both boldness and integrity for us when he stands before religious and political authorities in the book of Acts. Note the similarities in these two accounts of his defense:

> The commander wanted to find out exactly why Paul was being accused by the Jews. So the next day he released him and ordered the chief priests and all the members of the Sanhedrin to assemble. Then he brought Paul and had him stand before them. Paul looked straight at the Sanhedrin and said, "My brothers, I have fulfilled my duty to God in all *good conscience* to this day (Acts 22:30–23:1 TNIV, emphasis mine).

> When the governor [Felix] motioned for him to speak, Paul replied: "I know that for a number of years you have been a judge over this nation; so I gladly make my defense. . . . I admit that I worship the God of our fathers as a follower of the Way, which they call a sect. I believe everything that is in accordance with the Law and that is written in the Prophets, and I have the same hope in God as these people themselves have, that there will be a resurrection of both the righteous and the wicked. So I strive always to

keep my conscience clear before God and all people (Acts 24:10–17, TNIV, emphasis mine).

In both cases, Paul's defense includes a clear conscience. In the first defense, he says he carried out his life and ministry "in *all* good conscience." In the second one, Paul exclaims, "I *strive always* to keep my conscience clear *before God and all people.*" Paul zealously pursued a clear conscience in all things and exhorts others to do the same.

Having integrity means we strive for a clear conscience. And a clear conscience confirms our integrity. This kind of integrity gave Paul boldness and enabled him to live his life with authenticity. If we want to live and serve others with authenticity, we will continually pursue a clear conscience.

No matter what role people take in order to bless the communities where they live, whether they live in their home country or in foreign countries, they need to be able to fulfill that role with heartfelt integrity: "I am an English teacher-follower of Jesus for the glory of God"; "I am a businessperson-follower of Jesus for the glory of God"; "I am an aid worker-follower of Jesus for the glory of God." Their basic identity remains the same among all three audiences.

I love how my friend Chris Seiple describes it:

> Christians are intentional ambassadors of reconciliation who have been given the gift of vocation and location to live out Christ's love.... In other words, Christians cannot live their lives according to their vocation—even if it's full time ministry! We must be ambassadors of reconciliation first, ambassadors assigned a particular call. We are good neighbors who use our vocation—from Bible translation to electric engineering to military service to nursing—as an opportunity to be ambassadors of reconciliation.[1]

Even so, the liberating transparency of an integrated identity still requires wisdom. Jesus highlights this in his first commission to his disciples, "See, I am sending you out like sheep into the midst of wolves; so be wise as serpents and innocent as doves" (Matt 10:16). Jesus says that we are sent like defenseless sheep among ravenous wolves, vulnerable and in danger. We may not feel vulnerable or in danger if we live in certain Western countries, but this reflects the reality that many followers of Jesus experience in many countries around the world.

---

1. Seiple, "Christian Mission in Every Sphere."

An Integrated Identity

Because of this, Jesus exhorts us to imitate snakelike behavior. Snakes are camouflaged. They fit into their environment and maintain a low profile, not drawing attention to themselves. However, Jesus' followers are not just called to be snakelike "undercover agents." They are also called to be like doves—guileless and innocent. The innocence of integrity must be balanced by the wisdom of discretion. Snakelike behavior alone can degrade to deviousness; dovelike behavior alone can turn into gullibility. Followers of Jesus are called to both wisdom and guilelessness. Walking in integrity does not mean we reveal every aspect of our lives to everyone we meet.

The figure below helps illustrate what I am talking about. We each need to find our sweet spot at the center of the spectrum. Where the center is will differ with each person because of personality, gifting, calling, conscience, and context. But we are all called to find and live in the "both/and" tension of shrewdness and innocence, wisdom and integrity. In this way, we will experience the greatest liberty in living out and sharing the gospel.

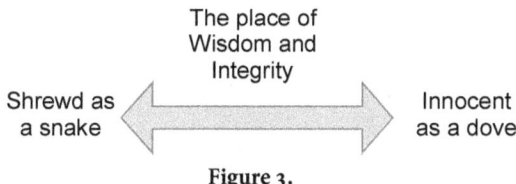

Figure 3.

An integrated identity has eluded many cross-cultural workers for at least three reasons: (1) outdated missionary paradigms, (2) dualistic views of life (the dichotomy between the sacred and secular—including our view of work), and (3) misunderstanding of "tentmaking" in the life of Paul.

Let's examine each of these hindrances and discern how twenty-first-century disciples of Christ can follow Jesus among neighbors and the nations with authenticity.

OUTDATED MISSIONARY PARADIGMS

One purpose of this book is to critique outdated missionary paradigms. The traditional missionary paradigm goes something like this. Dedicated followers of Jesus feel called to go to a far-off place to reach a group of people who have never heard of Christ. To do this they ask churches to support them—a "collection-plate economy" model of ministry. They get a missionary visa as full-time religious workers and ministers in their host country. They are mono-vocational and do formal, public ministry.

This traditional model has been modified most recently in what are known as restricted-access countries—countries perceived as hostile to the gospel. (I think these countries are primarily hostile to Christianity and its association with the West and not necessarily Jesus.) Instead of missionary visas they get secular visas, serve the Lord "part time," and do informal, private ministry. They see themselves as "tentmakers," imitating Paul the apostle (Acts 18:1–4), and thus are bi-vocational. Most of them don't spend much time actually working since they are also sent out from and supported by a local church. They call themselves tentmakers but in reality, many are tent-fakers. They are not doing real business, or they only work a few hours a week.

Again, I will illustrate from my own experience. I was an English teacher in Indonesia for over eight years. I actually had an MA in TESOL (Teaching English to Speakers of Other Languages) with a specialization in advanced reading. My thesis was on discourse analysis. Yet I only worked about ten hours a week as an English teacher. The rest of the time was for ministry or doctoral research. I actually received high marks on my English teaching according to student evaluations. But I did not put in the hours necessary for me to have real integrity in my work.

At that time I thought I was doing the right thing. I was living according to the standards of the evangelical scribes. But I now realize that I was not carrying out my good intentions in the right way. I did feel twinges of conscience back then. I assuaged my conscience, however, by telling myself I was doing this for the "cause." If I were coaching a young Rick Love today, I would make sure he put in a more appropriate amount of time and focused on excellence at work or found another role that really fit him.

So why do I say this traditional model reflects outdated paradigms? First, it is based on faulty assumptions and flawed foundations. It implicitly holds to a dualistic view of life and ministry. It also has distorted views of the Apostle Paul's tentmaking profession. (We address these topics in the chapters "Work, Worship, and Witness" and "Paul the Businessman-Follower of Jesus.")

Second, this traditional paradigm emerged when terrorism, pluralism, and globalization were not far-reaching global realities. Thus, it has not adjusted to the radically shrinking, interconnected world of the twenty-first century. Its practice reflects a compartmentalized, rather than a connected,

An Integrated Identity

view of the world. It fails to address the real-time, speed-of-light nature of today's communication.

NEW WINESKINS FOR A NEW ERA: THE GLOCAL-URBAN PARADIGM

The late Ralph Winter wrote a groundbreaking article called "Four Men, Three Eras." In it he described the history of modern missions as it relates to three different strategies or models of ministry. William Carey focused on the coastlands. Hudson Taylor challenged the church to go inland and founded the China Inland Mission. Cameron Townsend and Donald McGavran helped the church realize that the goal was not about geographical location but about reaching ethnic groups, or "unreached peoples."

By now it should be clear that I think we are in a new era that demands new paradigms. We are in the fourth era (following Ralph's paradigm). But before I continue, we need to look at one more important missiologist's view of history and mission paradigms. The late David J. Bosch's famous book, *Transforming Mission,* describes six different missiological paradigm shifts in the history of the church (see below).

1. The apocalyptic paradigm of primitive Christianity
2. The Hellenistic paradigm of the patristic period
3. The medieval Roman Catholic paradigm
4. The Protestant (Reformation) paradigm
5. The modern Enlightenment paradigm
6. The emerging ecumenical paradigm

Two decades ago, Bosch wrote:

> [W]e live in a period of transition, on the borderline between a paradigm that no longer satisfies and one that is, to a large extent, still amorphous and opaque. A time of paradigm change is, by nature, a time of crisis—a crisis, we remind ourselves, is the point where danger and opportunity meet.[2]

I believe we are now entering a new epoch and seventh missiological paradigm (following Bosch's typology). Like previous paradigms, it reflects

---

2. Bosch, *Transforming Mission,* 366.

a unique understanding of the Christian faith with its own distinctive missiology.

I call this the "glocal-urban paradigm." This paradigm heralds the centrality of two mega-trends: glocalization and urbanization. Glocalization is at the heart of this book and needs little mention here. Urbanization does not get a lot of press in this book, so I need to comment on it now.

Urbanization is one of the defining traits of the modern world. Over half the world now lives in cities! There are twenty-seven megacities in the world today with populations over ten million. There are more than 400 cities with populations over a million. Following Jesus into the cities of the world will lead us to culture shapers, unreached peoples, and the poorest of the poor. "The 21st Century will be the first urban century in history. This fact will affect every area of life, and mold the shape of Christian ministries in the future."[3]

Cities need to be our priority.

The glocal-urban paradigm helps us understand and minister effectively in this present era. This new paradigm sets the stage to address the hindrances to ministry in a glocalized world—the dichotomy between the sacred and secular, and a faulty understanding of tentmaking.

---

3. Johnstone, *The Future of the Global Church*, 6.

7

Work, Worship, and Witness

> Work is not a secular activity; it is a sacred one originally ordained by God, and so it must be undertaken in holy ways.
>
> BEN WITHERINGTON III

Pastors are spiritual. Businesspeople aren't. Prayer is spiritual. Work isn't. The unseen, heavenly realm is what counts. The physical world doesn't count. This sacred/secular dichotomy has plagued the church from the beginning.

This dualistic view of life is heresy (yes, heresy!) and it takes a toll on us. It keeps us from enjoying God's good gifts and robs us from finding satisfaction in our work. It often makes those of us who are not in "full-time, professional ministry" feel like second-class citizens in the kingdom of God. This viewpoint keeps followers of Christ from fruitfully engaging people in the workplace. It hinders the fulfillment of the Great Commission. This is bad news!

So why do so many Christians persist in embracing this false and crippling worldview?

One reason for this kind of split spirituality is a distorted, unbiblical view of the created world. God pronounced the physical world, his creation, as good (Gen 1:4, 10, 12, 18, 21, 25, 31). To deny the goodness of

God's creation is to deny the goodness of the Creator. This earthly existence is God's heavenly plan! We should see the handiwork of God in creation.

God also demonstrated his profound commitment to this earthly existence in the incarnation. God became flesh in Jesus (John 1:1, 14). Even in its fallen state, God sent Jesus into the world not to deliver us from the physical world, but to reconcile, heal, and restore all of creation.

Paul explicitly teaches against a sacred/secular dualism.

> Let the word of Christ dwell in you richly; teach and admonish one another in all wisdom; and with gratitude in your hearts sing psalms, hymns, and spiritual songs to God. And whatever you do, in word or deed, do everything in the name of the Lord Jesus, giving thanks to God the Father through him (Col 3:16–17).

Note the stark the contrast between these two verses (sentences). First Paul addresses how believers minister to one another through mutual sharing. No clergy. No hierarchy. Full participation. (It is easier to do this in house churches—which is where they gathered in Colossae.) This is the supposedly sacred part of life. This is the "church service." This is where we get spiritual.

But then, in the very next verse, Paul goes on to talk about the supposedly secular part of life. "*Whatever you do* in word or deed,"—which includes work!—"do everything in the name of the Lord Jesus." All of life counts for Jesus. Jesus doesn't just want to reign over our devotions or our church services. He wants to rule over all of life.

Elsewhere, Paul says, "So, whether you eat or drink, or *whatever you do*, do everything for the glory of God" (1 Cor 10:31, emphasis mine). Paul affirms that all of life can glorify God. The issue for Paul is not sacred versus secular. The issue is lordship and motivation. Will we submit all that we do to Christ? Will we seek to live with him and for him in all things?

One of the most damaging ways the sacred/secular dichotomy demonstrates itself is in the clergy/laity split. For example, the phrase "full-time Christian service" often denotes the superior quality of clerical or missionary work. Let's see what the Apostle Peter says about these issues.

> But you are a chosen race, a royal priesthood, a holy nation, God's own people, in order that you may proclaim the mighty acts of him who called you out of darkness into his marvelous light (1 Peter 2:9).

This verse describes what is known as the priesthood of all believers, a doctrine foundational to Protestantism. According to Peter, all believers are priests. It was this doctrine that motivated Reformers such as Martin Luther to talk about all good work done by Christians as ministry. There was no longer such thing as "super-Christians" and "regular Christians"; there were just Christians. In this way, Luther broke down the distinction between work in general and ministerial work in particular, or between sacred and secular work. Gene E. Veith makes a profound observation about the priesthood of all believers:

> The doctrine of vocation amounts to a comprehensive doctrine of the Christian life, having to do with faith and sanctification, grace and good works. It is a key to Christian ethics. It shows how Christians can influence culture. It transfigures ordinary, everyday life with the presence of God. . . . The priesthood of all believers did not make everyone into church workers; rather it turned every kind of work into a sacred calling.[1]

Work is sacred according to the Scriptures. As God's image bearers, Adam and Eve were commissioned to rule the earth as partners (Genesis 1:26–28). Their mission to rule the earth involved work. Genesis 2:15 makes this explicit: "The LORD God took the man and put him in the garden of Eden to till it and to keep it." Thus, prior to the fall and the curse, Adam and Eve worked. We were created to work, and work is good!

But we now live in a fallen world, under a curse. Work involves painful toil and sweat (Gen 3:17–19). So that means that work is bad now, right? Wrong. Work is harder because evil assaults our world. But sin does not make work inherently bad. God's commission to rule the earth still stands. Work remains part of God's good plan.

How can our work please God? How can our work be spiritual? A passage from Paul's letter to the Colossians guides us in this pursuit:

> Slaves, obey your earthly masters in everything, not only while being watched and in order to please them, but wholeheartedly, fearing the Lord. Whatever your task, put yourselves into it, as done for the Lord and not for your masters, since you know that from the Lord you will receive the inheritance as your reward; you serve the Lord Christ (Col 3:22–24).

---

1. Veith Jr., *God at Work*, 17, 19.

Part III: A Core Identity Worth Living For

Let me say a few things about slavery before I address what Paul teaches about work. Slavery is evil, but Paul did not confront the issue of slavery head-on for two reasons. First, the church was a persecuted minority in a hostile environment. Paul did not want the good news to be perceived as an attack on the status quo. Second, Paul saw the gospel working in society like leaven. So he encouraged slaves to be godly models and to serve the Lord wholeheartedly within their context (Eph 6:5–8; Col 3:22–25; 1 Cor 7:17–24, 29, 31, 35). He also urged just treatment of slaves by their masters (Eph 6:9; Col 4:1). Rather than use a direct approach as a prophet of justice, the apostle to the nations worked within society's structures to bring about transformation. Through word and deed he planted seeds which would ultimately undermine the unjust institution of slavery (Gal 3:28; Philemon).

In this context, what Paul teaches about work is profound. Even in the most horrible situations (such as slavery), God still considers work a good thing. Notice how Paul exhorts slaves to view their work. First, he reminds them to be conscientious workers—to be obedient in everything. Next, he calls them to carry out their toilsome duties as unto the Lord—with integrity and dedication, fearing and serving God. Finally, he encourages these oppressed laborers with an eternal perspective. The Lord will reward them.

In a parallel passage, Paul encourages slaves to promote the gospel through beautiful lives. "Slaves . . . must show themselves to be entirely trustworthy and good. Then they will make the teaching about God our Savior attractive in every way" (Titus 2:9–10, NLT). Work well done, with a positive attitude, becomes a winsome witness.

Paul explains how Christ's lordship works in real life. He exhorts slaves (and all workers) to a holistic rather than a dualistic view of the spiritual life. All of life is spiritual because the Lord is present. He encourages these slaves to be incarnational—to model the gospel where they live. We can please God even in the midst of oppressive work.

The sacred/secular dichotomy denies God's good creation; it denies Christ's lordship over all of life; and it denies the Holy Spirit's pervasive work in all spheres of life. That is wrong!

As followers of Christ, we embrace a holistic view of life, work, and ministry. All of life is sacred; all of life is devoted to Jesus. There is no such thing as "secular" from a biblical perspective. Whether as businesspeople, educators, mothers, fathers, relief and development workers, or whatever we do, we do it heartily to the Lord, for his honor.

Work, Worship, and Witness

Wherever we live and whatever our occupation, our work is witness. The quality of our work, the diligence of our labor, and the love demonstrated to our colleagues glorifies God (Matt 5:16). We make the gospel attractive by our good deeds (Titus 2:10). In fact, the beauty of our lives should demand an explanation, thus giving us an opportunity to speak of Jesus.

I think it's important to stop a moment and think about how this holistic view of life, work, and ministry relates to the average person in the pew. What are the implications of this for the vast majority of Jesus' followers around the world—those who do not see themselves as missionaries? These people don't work as a means to minister. They work to live. So they usually need to learn more about how they can be "good news people" on the job!

The missional church movement focuses on encouraging and equipping people like this. In many ways the theology and practice of the missional church overlaps greatly with the main themes of this book. Missional churches have five distinctives that highlight the integration of work and witness.

1. The whole church is sent into the world, not just a few missionaries. There are many churches that actively send missionaries but are not themselves missional because they do not believe that everyone in the church is a missionary.
2. The focus is not primarily on the church gathered on Sunday, but on the church scattered from Monday through Saturday. One of the major goals of the pastoral team is to train their members to be "missional" in their jobs—in every vocation and location.
3. The focus of the missional church is primarily on laity not preachers or professionals.
4. The focus is incarnational, understanding this as relevant communication and humble service. Church members understand that they represent Jesus' real presence in a divided, damaged world.
5. The focus is on understanding and communicating well with those outside the church.

Part III: A Core Identity Worth Living For

TOWARD AN INTEGRATED IDENTITY: WORK, WORSHIP, AND WITNESS

So how do we do this? How can we overcome a dualistic worldview and work toward having an integrated identity worth living for? How can we see that work, worship, and witness should be seamless in our lives?

I have four suggestions. First, there is a broad spectrum of legitimate types of work. We have to admit that all work is not created equal. Some jobs more readily reflect the values and priorities of the kingdom than others. Certain types of work potentially bring God more glory than others. So we need to be discerning about the kinds of work we do (if our situation and the economic climate allow us these options).

Being a janitor is legitimate work. Selling illegal drugs is not. But most of life is not a choice between good and evil. We usually choose between good and better, or at times between good and best. How we discern this is explained in the next suggestion.

Second, we need to recognize that we are stewards of the gifts and resources God gives us. Through work we exercise dominion and faithful stewardship. Jesus put a strong emphasis on being a good steward and being productive (Matt 25:14-30; Luke 19:11-27). Thus any position, whether pastor, CEO, teacher, janitor, aid worker, or salesperson, may or may not be good stewardship of your particular gifts. You need to find the kind of profession that maximizes your potential for good. Discerning a profession like this is often an ongoing process where you evaluate your skills, examine your passions, and assess your opportunities.

Third, we glorify God through our work when we have the right heart motivation. This leads us to the role of spiritual disciplines again. A beautiful life flows from habits of the heart. Through prayer and hiding God's word in our hearts, the everyday tasks of our lives can be set apart for his purposes. We pray: "Jesus, I want to follow you today in my job. Guide me. Purify my heart. Let the words of my mouth and the mediations of my heart please you. Show me how to serve my co-workers. May my actions and attitudes reflect your love."

Fourth, the whole church is sent, not just a few missionaries. God wants to have his people bearing witness in every vocation and location. This can only happen if God's people work in every sector of the city with a sense of divine purpose.

It is commonplace among some evangelical leaders to talk about domains of culture. "In 1975, Campus Crusade for Christ founder Bill Bright and Youth With A Mission (YWAM) founder Loren Cunningham came together and identified what they called 'Seven Mountains of Influence'—pillars or domains of society that need to be transformed."[2] These domains include the following:

1. Education
2. Arts and Entertainment
3. Government
4. Religion
5. Family
6. Media
7. Business

God's people are naturally deployed across all domains of culture. Followers of Jesus connect to society in these natural infrastructures of the city. The gospel is incarnated through normal work in the various spheres. This makes work holy and leads to an integrated identity worth living for!

---

2. Swanson and Williams, *To Transform a City*, 150.

8

Paul the Businessman-Follower of Jesus

> The secular job is not an inconvenience, but the God-given context in which tentmakers live out the gospel in a winsome, wholesome, non-judgmental way, demonstrating personal integrity, doing quality work and developing caring relationships.
>
> RUTH SIEMANS

If you ask the average Christian to describe the Apostle Paul, they would probably say something about his great missionary work. He was an apostle. Others may portray Paul more as a theologian. He wrote twelve of the letters that were included in the New Testament. But I doubt if anyone would describe Paul as a businessman—even though he made tents to support himself (Acts 18:3).

A cursory reading of the New Testament may seem to indicate that Paul spent very little time actually making tents. But is this really the case?

Was he a full-time Christian worker who made tents only when he needed money? Actually, there is clear biblical evidence that he made tents on all three of his journeys and that tentmaking played a central role in his ministry. Paul was a businessman-follower of Jesus.

Paul viewed his work and ministry as integrated. Tentmaking was no "cover" or mere "platform" for Paul. He was no job-faker. Certainly, his apostolic calling was the driving force of his life. Paul did all things for the sake of the gospel (1 Cor 9:23). But just as certainly, work played a central role in the fulfillment of his calling.

The New Testament does not provide enough evidence about Paul's tentmaking to draw indisputable conclusions about how much time he worked. Some who are pro-tentmaking will go beyond the evidence to make their point, while others who see tentmaking as insignificant will minimize the evidence. Let's examine the evidence afresh, and you draw your own conclusions.

PAUL'S APOSTOLIC JOURNEYS

First apostolic journey.

The book of Acts does not describe Paul's tentmaking activities during his first journey (Acts 13–14). However, Paul clearly alludes to it in his discussion about his rights as an apostle: "I and Barnabas . . . *must work for a living*" (1 Cor 9:6, NIV, emphasis mine). This indicates that Paul worked to support himself on his first journey since he teamed up with Barnabas only on his first journey.

Second apostolic journey.

Both Acts and the Epistles mention Paul's tentmaking activities on this journey. Acts 17 describes Paul's ministry to the Thessalonians, and both Letters to the Thessalonians describe his long hours and arduous work doing manual labor.

> You remember our labor and toil, brothers and sisters; we worked night and day, so that we might not burden any of you while we proclaimed to you the gospel of God (1 Thess 2:9).

> For you yourselves know how you ought to imitate us; we were not idle when we were with you, and we did not eat anyone's bread without paying for it; but with toil and labor we worked night and day, so that we might not burden any of you. This was not because we do not have that right, but in order to give you an example to imitate (2 Thess 3:7–9).

We can draw a number of significant conclusions about work (tentmaking) and following Jesus among neighbors and nations from these passages:

1. Paul worked hard and put in long hours in his secular occupation. In the poignant words of the late president of Fuller Seminary, David Hubbard: "Aching arms, tired fingers, calloused hands were a daily experience for this tentmaker. He paid a high price for his integrity. But he felt it was worth the price to fulfill Christ's mission."[1]

2. Paul made tents to serve as an example to others. Perhaps he aimed to challenge the commonly held aversion for manual labor held by many Greeks. But certainly, "Paul regarded idleness, which was endemic in Greco-Roman society, as inappropriate for the Christian believer. So he deliberately set the example of hard work to support himself and called upon his [followers] to imitate him."[2]

3. He did not see his work as a distraction from his calling as an apostle. New Testament scholar Gordon Fee makes this observation about Paul's tentmaking: "At least as early as the mission to Thessalonica, what was originally a necessity had developed into a studied expression of his mission."[3]

Ronald Hock has probably published more research on Paul's tentmaking than any other New Testament scholar. He has shown that far from being peripheral to Paul's apostolic calling, tentmaking was an integral part of it. "More than any of us has supposed, Paul was *Paul the Tentmaker*. His trade occupied much of his time. . . . [H]is life was very much that of the workshop . . . of being bent over a workbench like a slave and of working side by side with slaves."[4]

---

1. Hubbard, *Thessalonians*, 22–23.
2. Barnett, "Tentmaking."
3. Fee, *The First Epistle to the Corinthians*, 179; see also 1 Thessalonians 2:9, 4:11; 2 Thessalonians 3:6–13.
4. Hock, *The Social Context of Paul's Mission*, 67.

Paul's work at Corinth is the most explicit and detailed description of his work as a tentmaker.

> There he found a Jew named Aquila, a native of Pontus, who had recently come from Italy with his wife Priscilla, because Claudius had ordered all Jews to leave Rome. Paul went to see them, and, because he was of the same trade, he stayed with them, and they worked together—by trade they were tentmakers. Every sabbath he would argue in the synagogue and would try to convince Jews and Greeks. When Silas and Timothy arrived from Macedonia, Paul was occupied with proclaiming the word, testifying to the Jews that the Messiah was Jesus (Acts 18:2–5).

Paul began his ministry at Corinth by working as a tentmaker during the week with Aquila and Priscilla. "Every sabbath"—implying some sort of routine—Paul would minister in the synagogue. After an unspecified period of time, Silas and Timothy brought a financial gift from the Philippian church in Macedonia (Phil 4:14–15). This enabled Paul to stop the work of making tents and reprioritize his time to minister in other ways. Though Paul's apostolic modus operandi was tentmaking, he also accepted financial support so that he could give more time to discipleship and leadership training. In addition, accepting support enabled the churches to participate with Paul in his ministry. Paul's concern was for the giver as much as for the gift (Phil 4:17).

Third apostolic journey.

Paul's farewell address to the Ephesian elders in Acts 20:34–35 makes it clear that Paul worked as a tentmaker during his ministry at Ephesus. Imagine Paul sharing his heart with the Ephesian leaders. He lifts up his calloused hands and says:

> You know for yourselves that I worked with my own hands to support myself and my companions. In all this I have given you an example that by such work we must support the weak, remembering the words of the Lord Jesus, for he himself said, "It is more blessed to give than to receive."

Paul's hands made tents to support himself, to meet the needs of his team, and to model hard work for the sake of the emerging church. At Ephesus, Paul's tentmaking and apostleship were a seamless whole:

Some Greek manuscripts indicate that Paul had the use of the building of Tyrannus from 11 A.M. to 4 P.M. Tyrannus no doubt held his classes in the early morning. Public activity ceased in the cities of Ionia for several hours at 11 A.M., and . . . more people would be asleep at 1 P.M. than at 1 A.M. But Paul, after spending the early hours of the day working making tents, devoted the midday hours of burden and heat working at his exhausting business of teaching and discipling. His zeal and energy were such that he must have infected his hearers, so that they were willing to sacrifice their siesta for the sake of listening to Paul.[5]

Hock argues that "the workshop was a recognized social setting in Paul's day for intellectual discourse."[6] Thus, Paul's demanding schedule allowed time for both tentmaking and teaching, and his work as a tentmaker enabled him to share the gospel freely in the context of his work. In other words, his tentmaking job enhanced his gospel-planting effectiveness.

PAUL'S BACKGROUND AND TRAINING: AN INTEGRATED VIEW OF WORK AND MINISTRY.

As a rabbi (Acts 22:3), Paul would have been trained both in the Scriptures and in a secular trade to support his ministry.

The importance of this bi-vocational emphasis is reflected in rabbinic traditions. Rabbi Gamaliel declared, "An excellent thing is the study of the Torah combined with some worldly occupation, for the labor demanded by them both makes sin to be forgotten. All study of the Torah without work must in the end be futile and become the cause of sin."[7]

Though trained as a Jewish rabbi, Paul was an apostle to the Gentiles (Rom 11:13). Thus it is important to understand the social and intellectual milieu of the Greek world in which he served. Wandering itinerant Hellenistic philosophers were common in Paul's day. These philosophers supported themselves in different ways. Some begged, others charged fees, accepted patronage, or supported themselves by working.

Both his rabbinic background and models from the Greek world indicate that Paul practiced a seamless approach to ministry. He was trained in

---

5. Bruce, *Commentary on the Book of Acts*, 388–89.
6. "The Workshop," 450.
7. Aboth II, 2, in Montefiore and Loewe, eds., *A Rabbinic Anthology*, 175.

both secular and sacred work and saw life, work, and ministry as a seamless whole. Work was witness and he witnessed at work.

GUIDING PRINCIPLES FOR PAUL'S APOSTLESHIP AND TENTMAKING

Paul was apparently criticized at Corinth for working and not accepting financial support. His unwillingness to accept patronage had been misinterpreted and used as an argument against him. Thus, in 1 Corinthians 9:3, Paul defends his apostleship: "This is my defense to those who would examine me." In the rest of the chapter, Paul explains some of his guiding principles on apostleship and doing business as missions.

First, he argues for the "rights" of an apostle. In a series of cascading questions and multiple metaphors he drives home his point. Soldiers, farmers, shepherds, priests, and even oxen all receive remuneration for their labors. He clinches his argument by appealing to a word from Jesus: "the Lord has commanded that those who preach the Gospel should receive their living from the Gospel" (1 Cor 9:14, NIV).

Nevertheless, Paul renounces this God-given right. Several times in this chapter he states emphatically:

> If others have this right of support from you, shouldn't we have it all the more? But we did not use this right. On the contrary, we put up with anything rather than hinder the Gospel of Christ (1 Cor 9:12, NIV).

"What then is my reward? Just this: that in my proclamation I may make the gospel free of charge, so as not to make full use of my rights in the gospel" (1 Cor 9:18).

Why did Paul work as a tentmaker and voluntarily relinquish his rights to be supported as an apostle? The historical context in which Paul worked gives us valuable insight. Paul's adamant refusal to accept support almost certainly stands in contrast to the practices of the itinerant philosophers who peddled their wisdom or religious instruction for monetary gain.

This much is clear about Paul's situation in Corinth—he felt that receiving support from those he was ministering to, instead of working to support himself, would adversely impact the work of the gospel. Thus, Paul did not accept the patronage of the Corinthians, so that he could blamelessly proclaim the gospel. It was an issue of credibility. He wanted to be a pro bono preacher!

For Paul, tentmaking was a non-negotiable part of his apostolic calling. The full-time ministry of the word was not Paul's highest ministry consideration. His greatest concern was to minister the word with integrity and credibility.

INSIGHTS FROM PAUL'S EXPERIENCE

Paul worked as a tentmaker out of necessity. Though he was supported by some churches some of the time, he did not have the luxury of regular gifts from churches. Most of the time, he needed to work to support himself and his team.

Paul also worked as a tentmaker for the sake of credibility. He was willing to labor for long hours at his trade rather than be accused of impure financial motives. He also worked hard as a tentmaker so that he could preach the gospel without feeling obligated to a patron, thereby jeopardizing his freedom to teach the truth.

Paul the tentmaker/apostle modeled an integrated identity, for at least three reasons:

1. His training as a rabbi helped him embrace seamless ministry.
2. For Paul, all of life was devoted to God. Hence, his theology was not confused by a secular-sacred dichotomy.
3. As a tentmaker, Paul was able to share his faith in the context of his work. His job helped him live out an integrated identity as an apostle.

Paul's model of tentmaking is reproducible. Churches in most developing countries do not have the financial capacity to follow a Western model of donor support. Even if they did, tentmaking would remain the model that can be imitated by the greatest number of new workers.

Paul's tentmaking enhanced his disciple-making effectiveness. Paul's work as a tentmaker enabled him to share the gospel freely in the context of his work. This is not true about all tentmaking. Some jobs facilitate the forming of communities of Jesus' followers and others do not. For example, when I first lived in Indonesia, I taught English to ethnic Chinese young people. However, I was seeking to share Jesus with the Sundanese. If I were starting over today, I would look harder for a working environment that would put me in daily contact with the Sundanese.

There are important similarities between Paul's tentmaking and ours today. Both Paul and today's workers are "tentmakers" for the sake of the gospel. Both Paul and today's tentmakers do tentmaking out of necessity: Paul's need was financial; today's workers often need a legitimate visa. Like Paul, we seek credibility in the community and to integrate our faith in everything we do. Finally, both Paul and most tentmakers today also receive some financial support from churches (Phil 4:15).

There are also significant differences. Motivation for modern tentmaking has been initially focused on procuring visas so the gospel can be communicated in countries that do not issue missionary visas. Paul saw his business ministry and teaching ministry as one. Another major difference between Paul and modern apostles is cultural and linguistic distance. Paul did not have to learn another language. He could minister in Greek. While he faced different cultural contexts, they were more similar to his than what most tentmakers face today. Practically, this means that modern tentmakers need to invest more time in one place working and ministering than Paul did. No other factor enhances a worker's ability to minister more than language fluency. Research has shown that tentmakers who work and learn the language simultaneously do not learn the language well. So, during the intensive period of language and culture learning, those who follow Jesus to the nations should find a way to give focused time to language learning if at all possible.

Paul the apostle's "old" paradigm of tentmaker/apostle (applied more rigorously than it is in most organizations) offers surprising hope for "new" paradigms of ministry in the twenty-first century.

COMMUNICATING OUR CORE MESSAGE AND INTEGRATED IDENTITY

I want to close this chapter with a passage that guides us in both communicating our core message and living out our core identity:

> But in your hearts revere Christ as Lord. Always be prepared to give an answer to everyone who asks you to give the reason for the hope that you have. But do this with gentleness and respect, keeping a clear conscience, so that those who speak maliciously against

Part III: A Core Identity Worth Living For

your good behavior in Christ may be ashamed of their slander (1 Pet 3:15–16, NIV).

First notice what Peter says about the "what" of our core message—that is, the hope we have in Christ. Communicating our core message demands diligent preparation ("always be prepared") and rigorous thought ("give the reason"). Understanding how to share the good news about Jesus in relevant, compelling ways doesn't come easily. Even as I write this chapter I am preparing for a conference—by reading and thinking deeply about the best way to share what my faith means.

Second, Peter exhorts us about the "how" of our core message. He urges us to communicate our message with both gentleness and respect. In other words, communication involves both our wording and our being. Gentleness and respect are habits of the heart that we must cultivate. Gentleness implies that we share without arrogance or pushiness, and respect implies that we show honor. Please note: speaking gently and respectfully is not about being politically correct—it is about following apostolic mandate. Our websites, sermons, and personal lives should always display these twin virtues.

Third, Peter points out that ministry demands integrity. Note that this passage begins with an exhortation to revere Christ as Lord "in our hearts" and ends with the plea to "keep a clear conscience." To communicate with integrity to all three of our audiences demands an inside-out ethic of heart change.

Fourth, Peter indicates that sharing our faith grows out of relationship with others. We are called to "give an answer." If someone asks me for the hope that is within me, that means that we have a relationship. They know what makes me tick. They see something winsome or unique in my life that interests them. (Or maybe they just think I'm weird.)

I like how *The Message* translates this verse: "Through thick and thin, keep your hearts at attention, in adoration before Christ, your Master. Be ready to speak up and tell anyone who asks why you're living the way you are, and always with the utmost courtesy."

Peter assumes we live lives worth questioning. The quality of our lives should demand an explanation. In the context of friendship we show and share the love of Jesus with integrity, gentleness, and respect.

We have a core message worth dying for and an integrated identity worth living for.

PART IV

A Core Dream Worth Suffering For

9

Blessing All Nations

The Abrahamic covenant is a moral agenda for God's people as well as a mission statement by God.

CHRISTOPHER J. H. WRIGHT

I spoke in a church where a member told me that we need to "conquer" the world for Christ! Conquer? This military metaphor certainly doesn't remind me of Jesus. It is another example of the kind of triumphalistic language that really bothers me. Like the imperialism or colonialism of the past, it betrays the good news we seek to share.

It isn't just overtly militant language that compromises our message. Some of the more innocuous (to us) ways that we frame our global vision can distort the good news. For example, a number of years ago, I was flying to Ireland to speak at a missions convention. A doctoral student named Muhammad sat next to me. Our conversation was positive and stimulating as we discussed a number of spiritual and political topics. I was relaxed as I explained to Muhammad that I was speaking at a Christian conference. But suddenly it hit me. In the folder on my lap was a flyer about a missionary conference with me as the keynote speaker. I did my best not to let the flyer fall out! This incident illustrates the tensions we face.

What would my friend Muhammad think if he saw the flyer promoting this "missionary conference." He might wonder if this conference was

Part IV: A Core Dream Worth Suffering For

aimed at aggressive proselytism and the promotion of Western imperialism, or if it was focused on defaming Islam. As I sat next to my Muslim acquaintance, I thought how much better it would be if the theme of the conference was "blessing the nations."

THE DREAM OF BLESSING ALL NATIONS

Martin Luther King, Jr. had a dream. Do you? What is your vision for the world? What themes or metaphors provide a comprehensive, biblically faithful, and positive summary of God's dream for the world? How do we then embrace and communicate that dream to our three main audiences all at once (see figure 4)?

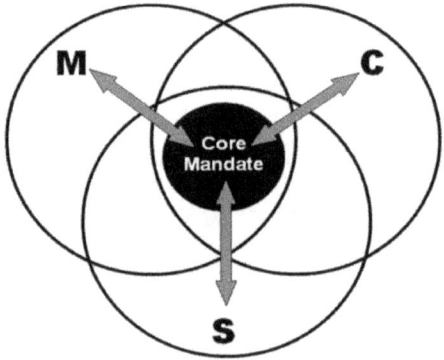

Figure 4.
3D Communication: Core Mandate

God's dream for the world (our global mandate) has been described in many ways in the past: "fulfilling the Great Commission," "obeying Christ's last command," "reaching the unreached," "seeking the lost," and "rescuing the perishing." Every church and every organization needs to discern how they will describe this dream for themselves.

The scriptural theme of "blessing all nations" provides a profound way to explain a global dream worth suffering for.

> Now the Lord said to Abram, "Go from your country and your kindred and your father's house to the land that I will show you. I will make of you a great nation, and I will bless you, and make your name great, so that you will be a blessing. I will bless those who bless you, and the one who curses you I will curse; and in you all the families of the earth shall be blessed" (Genesis 12:1–3).

This passage describes a turning point in history. The arrogance of the human heart displayed in the building of the tower of Babel in Genesis 11 led to God's judgment. Humanity became divided and dispersed. So what was God's plan for a diverse people alienated from him and one another? Mission leading to blessing.

The Abrahamic revolution stared with a call to go! A call to obey the God of all the families and cultures of the world. God commissioned Abraham to bring healing to this divided and broken world by promising to bless all nations through him. God made his point by repeating the term *blessing* five times in this short passage. He also mentioned this promise to bless all nations five times in Genesis (Gen 12:1–3, 18:18, 22:18, 26:4, and 28:14).

The promise of blessing points forward to the new things God will do on earth. It also points backward to the original purpose that God had for all humanity. The promise of blessing connects the Abrahamic mandate with the original creation mandate:

> Then God said, "Let us make humankind in our image, according to our likeness; and let them have dominion over the fish of the sea, and over the birds of the air, and over the cattle, and over all the wild animals of the earth, and over every creeping thing that creeps upon the earth."
>
> So God created humankind in his image,
> in the image of God he created them;
> male and female he created them.
>
> God blessed them, and God said to them, "Be fruitful and multiply, and fill the earth and subdue it; and have dominion over the fish of the sea and over the birds of the air and over every living thing that moves upon the earth" (Gen 1:26–28).

"The LORD God took the man and put him in the garden of Eden to till it and to keep it" (Gen 2:15).

This original commission is sometimes called the creation mandate for two reasons. First, it was given at creation and second because it is a command to create. In the beginning, God created us, blessed us, and commissioned us. As God's image bearers our mandate is to rule the earth—to fill the earth and to cultivate and care for the environment (Gen 1:26–28, 2:15). We have a sacred stewardship.

The term *image* underscores the similarity between God and humanity. Just as ancient kings would erect an image of themselves to indicate their claim to dominion, so too humanity reflects God's image on earth, representing him and ruling on his behalf. Just as God rules in heaven, so too humanity rules on earth.

Thus, the Abrahamic mandate connects the original blessings of creation with the future promise of blessing the nations. God's work of redemption in Abraham is ultimately the restoration of God's original plan in creation. God's original creation purposes never change.

Now back to the future . . .

In the Abrahamic blessing, God describes his desire to overcome all forms of racism or tribalism. God's loving purpose includes all the ethnic groups of the earth. Here is the first mention of the Great Commission in Scripture. The theme of blessing the nations articulates the scope of our mandate and the proper heart attitude for ministry. We are not called to conquer, but commissioned to bless. God's dream for the whole world is blessing.

Genesis 12:1–3 helps us grasp the big picture of what God is doing in the world today. It provides a window into the meaning of the whole Bible. It is a pivotal text that binds the whole story of redemption together. Whereas Genesis 3—11 describes the bad news—human rebellion, arrogance, and division—Genesis 12 provides the good news of God's blessing and ultimate redemption (Gal 3:1–14). Genesis 3–11 portrays the problem that the rest of the Bible, Genesis 12—Revelation 22, addresses. The blessing of Abraham centers around three great themes:

- The promise of a land (Gen 12:1, 13:15, 15:7, and 17:8)
- The promise of a seed (Gen 12:2, 13:15, 15:5, and 17:4–5)
- The promise of universal blessing (Gen 12:3, 18:18, 22:18, 26:4, and 28:14)

The "promised land" provides much of the drama of the Old Testament. In many ways, the whole Old Testament centers on Israel and the land. Israel enters the promised land under Joshua, is expelled from the land because of disobedience, and returns to the promised land after exile.

The promise of a seed also provides dramatic moments early in the Old Testament story, because Abraham's wife, Sarah, was barren. After an excruciating number of years, God finally intervened, and Sarah gave birth to Isaac. Through Isaac, the promised seed grew and expanded into the nation of Israel. But ultimately, this promise found fulfillment in the New

Blessing All Nations

Testament through Jesus the Messiah, the son of Abraham (Matt 1:1; Gal 3:16).

So what about the promise of universal blessing? There are rare moments when the nations are explicitly blessed through Israel in the Old Testament. Egypt was blessed through Joseph, Babylon through Daniel, and Nineveh through Jonah. Usually, however, Israel was struggling to get its own act together. In spite of this, God continued to challenge his people about his dream to bless all peoples. The "all peoples" perspective of the Abrahamic narrative echoes throughout the Hebrew Scriptures.

But the full universalizing of this blessing takes place in the New Testament. Jesus is the "savior of the world" (John 4:42) who commissions his followers to make disciples of all nations (Matt 28:18–20). The blessing goes global.

In one his earliest sermons, the Apostle Peter argues that the gospel of Jesus fulfills the promise of Abraham:

> And all the prophets, as many as have spoken, from Samuel and those after him, also predicted these days. You are the descendants of the prophets and of the covenant that God gave to your ancestors, saying to Abraham, "And in your descendants all the families of the earth shall be blessed." When God raised up his servant, he sent him first to you, to bless you by turning each of you from your wicked ways (Acts 3:24–26).

According to the book of Revelation, Jesus' death on the cross guarantees the fulfillment of the promise to Abraham. Every nation will be blessed. God's global dream will come true:

> They sing a new song:
> "You are worthy to take the scroll
> and to open its seals,
> for you were slaughtered and by your blood you ransomed for God
> saints from every tribe and language and people and nation
> (Rev 5:9).

For some people the term *blessing* may seem old fashioned, out of touch with the twenty-first century. I am afraid that this massively important term has been drained of its power. Its meaning has been diluted because of superficial familiarity. "Oh Lord, bless the missionaries." That is the kind of thing we might hear a mom pray with her children. It sounds so simple, cute, and somehow right. Yet, the weight of heavenly power and heart-soothing comfort have been lost.

The Bible refers to blessing about 500 times! You don't have to be a scholar to realize that this is a central theme. Moreover, the quest for blessing is an almost universal longing among the peoples of the world.

Blessing refers to God's gracious favor and power bestowed on all humanity (Gen 30:27; Heb 6:7; cf. Luke 17:12–18), and in its fullest manifestation toward those who respond to him by faith (Gen 15:6; Eph 1:3; Gal 3:8; Ps 67). Favor and power? Who doesn't want that?

The blessing of God's favor draws us into relationship with himself. He promises to be our God (Gen 17:7–8). The result? Peace, well-being, salvation, and human flourishing. The blessing of his power impacts the practical realities of life, resulting in good harvests, long life, wealth, children, and miraculous works. Because of God's grace, nonbelievers experience the blessing of his power (Matt 5:45)—often through believers (for example, Jacob, Gen 30:27, 33:11; and Joseph, Gen 39:2–6).

But blessing includes more than receiving his favor and enjoying his power. We are blessed to be a blessing. The promise of blessing in Abraham includes doing justice.

> The Lord said, "Shall I hide from Abraham what I am about to do, seeing that Abraham shall become a great and mighty nation, and all the nations of the earth shall be blessed in him? No, for I have chosen him, that he may charge his children and his household after him to keep the way of the Lord by doing righteousness and justice; so that the Lord may bring about for Abraham what he has promised him" (Gen 18:17–19).

God chose Abraham to direct his children and household to keep the way of the Lord. And what is the content of this ethical curriculum? Doing what is right and just. In other words, God's promise to Abraham is intended to produce a community committed to social justice. Blessing the nations involves working for justice and righteousness!

THE CORE MESSAGE AND GLOBAL DREAM ARE ONE

God's promise to bless all nations in Abraham finds fulfillment in the New Testament. Paul's letter to the Galatians makes this explicit. In Galatians

Blessing All Nations

3:6–14 Paul describes the priority of Abraham and the Abrahamic blessing in the grand narrative of Scripture. In fact, in Galatians 3:6–8 Paul describes the gospel in terms of the Abrahamic blessing.

> Consider Abraham: "He believed God, and it was credited to him as righteousness." Understand, then, that those who believe are children of Abraham. The Scripture foresaw that God would justify the Gentiles by faith, and announced *the gospel in advance* to Abraham: "All nations will be blessed through you." So those who have faith are blessed along with Abraham, the man of faith (Gal 3:6–9, NIV, emphasis mine).

The Apostle Paul teaches that Abraham modeled what it means to "live by faith" with the result that he was considered "righteous." He was justified before God—"the exact opposite of being condemned by Him. [To be justified] is to be declared righteous, to be accepted, to stand in His favour and under His smile."[1]

Paul describes the concept of blessing all nations as "good news"—the gospel in advance! This implies that the good news includes both personal experience (blessing for myself) and global mandate (my responsibility to be a blessing to all nations). The message (blessing in Christ) and the mandate (to share this blessing with all nations) have become one.

Understanding the nature of our commission to bless is crucial in a glocalized world. Because of terrorism, stories of violence, hatred, and fear splash across the headlines daily. Diplomacy and the use of force should play an important role in governments' resistance to terrorism, but they often only escalate the violence. Polarization between Muslims and the West, or Muslims and Christians, increases daily. So we need to be people of blessing.

Some may ask, "Does the concept of 'blessing' work with all three audiences? Is it really three dimensional (3D)? It certainly works with Christians. They get it. But what about Muslims? Anyone who has any experience with Muslims will tell you that Muslims everywhere long for *baraka* (the Arabic term for blessing). I don't have much personal experience with Hindus or Buddhists, but I can't imagine that they wouldn't be drawn to blessing.

Some may think blessing sounds too sentimental or heavenly minded for secular audiences, so it's therefore only two dimensional (2D). However, I often hear the word *blessed* or *blessing* used on television in the US.

---

1. Stott, *The Message of Galatians*, 76.

Part IV: A Core Dream Worth Suffering For

I believe "the quest to attain a state of blessedness is a universal human longing."[2]

The word *blessing* speaks of favor with others, abundance, and success in life. Blessing is another way of talking about human flourishing. The secular person understands that! And the secular world does take notice of believers who truly model the gospel. Seeing the holistic ministry of evangelicals around the world has led secular journalist Nicolas Kristof of *The New York Times* to describe evangelicals positively as the "new internationalists."[3]

As the new internationalists, evangelicals bring the following blessings:

- Enjoying a personal relationship with God through faith in Christ and sharing that good news with others
- Experiencing God's power (in some measure) in all areas of life
- Working for social justice

As I will explain, the global dream of blessing all nations is about sharing Jesus, working for justice, and pursuing peace. It involves freeing slaves, ending poverty, and tending creation. This dream includes a variety of individuals, churches, and organizations working together—each fulfilling their unique part of the dream. And Jesus is at the center.

A GLOBAL DREAM WORTH SUFFERING FOR

The spread of blessing does not go uncontested. We face opposition. We struggle against the spiritual forces of darkness. I was shocked and brokenhearted to hear of the death of one of my colleagues in Somalia a number of years ago. This courageous man was shot at point-blank range in his car. He was a martyr who paid the ultimate price for Jesus.

I used to think that suffering meant things like martyrdom, imprisonment, physical beatings, or getting kicked out of a country for sharing the good news. It certainly does include these things. But suffering is usually much more mundane—leaving family and friends in obedience to God's call, getting out of our comfort zones, living in strange places, eating foods we don't like and enduring sickness, dying daily to our selfish desires. Whatever causes us pain is a form of suffering. Following Jesus among our

---

2. Ryken et al., *Dictionary of Biblical Imagery*.
3. Kristof, "Following God Abroad."

neighbors in our country of origin or in foreign countries, and working toward our global dream often results in suffering.

In both his Gospel and in Acts, Luke makes a clear connection between suffering and blessing the nations. Note the parallels between Jesus, Jesus' sent one (Paul), and Jesus' followers.

> Then he said to them, "Oh, how foolish you are, and how slow of heart to believe all that the prophets have declared! Was it not necessary that *the Messiah should suffer* these things and then enter into his glory?" Then beginning with Moses and all the prophets, he interpreted to them the things about himself in all the scriptures (Luke 24:25–27, emphasis mine).

> But the Lord said to him, "Go, for he is an instrument whom I have chosen to bring my name before Gentiles and kings and before the people of Israel; I myself will show him how much *he must suffer* for the sake of my name" (Acts 9:15–16, emphasis mine).

> After they had proclaimed the good news to that city and had made many disciples, they returned to Lystra, then on to Iconium and Antioch. There they strengthened the souls of the disciples and encouraged them to continue in the faith, saying, "It is through *many persecutions* that we must enter the kingdom of God." And after they had appointed elders for them in each church, with prayer and fasting they entrusted them to the Lord in whom they had come to believe (Acts 14:21–23, emphasis mine).

Luke uses the same Greek word in each of these passages—*dei*—to show that suffering "must" take place. Jesus had to suffer. Paul had to suffer. Jesus followers have to suffer (go "through many persecutions").

The Bible teaches it. Experience confirms it. Stories of persecution and suffering of Christians around the world make grim reading. Open Doors, for example, claims that "100 million Christians in over 60 countries are persecuted for their faith."[4]

But "the Abrahamic covenant *is* a moral agenda for God's people as well as a mission statement by God."[5]

That's why it is a global dream worth suffering for!

---

4. *Open Doors* website.
5. Wright, *The Mission of God*, 358, emphasis mine.

10

Blessing and Human Rights

Promoting religious freedom for all people must be an essential part of Christian mission in the twenty-first century.

JOSHUA DANESHFOROOZ

I can imagine my response as a young believer if someone had told me I needed to be concerned about human rights. I would have smugly said something like this: "I'm not concerned about human rights. I'm concerned about human wrongs!" Back then I understood that we are sinners. Now I realize that we are *also* the sinned against.

I am still concerned about human wrongs, but I've learned a few things. I now realize that it's wrong *not* to affirm human rights! Jesus' ethical demands—to love your neighbor as yourself and to do unto others as you would have them do unto you—make human rights a priority. So does the commission to bless all nations. As mentioned previously, blessing the nations includes teaching people the way of the Lord and working for justice and righteousness (Gen 18:19).

The most famous human rights document—*The Universal Declaration of Human Rights*—"has achieved the status of being a creed for the guidance of the nations. Affirmed officially today by more than 180 nations, it is the most widely adopted document in the world."[1] This weighty declaration is written in purely secular terms. However, there is a robust biblical basis of human rights that undergirds and shapes the moral foundations of this famous declaration. Let's look at one human right as an example of what blessing the nations encompasses: religious freedom.

THE BIBLICAL BASIS FOR FREEDOM OF RELIGION

"Is freedom of religion a liberal political agenda or is it a biblical mandate?" The middle-aged man sitting across from me asked this question intently in response to my comments on the role of religious freedom in peacemaking. I smiled and said, "Good question."

Here's how freedom of religion is described in Article 18: "Everyone has the right to freedom of thought, conscience and religion; this right includes freedom to change his religion or belief, and freedom, either alone or in community with others and in public or private, to manifest his religion or belief in teaching, practice, worship and observance."

I have to admit that there are no direct commands about freedom of religion in the Bible. But the Bible's call to imitate God and obey his commands has direct relevance to this issue (Eph 5:1; 1 John 5:3). The biblical doctrine of humanity being created in God's image and the biblical mandate to pursue justice also provide a basis for religious freedom.

Here are six reasons why I believe freedom of religion is a biblical mandate:

1. Freedom of religion is based on the creation story.

    God gave Adam and Eve freedom to obey or not to obey his commands (Gen 1–3). Because God wanted them to choose to love and obey him, he gave them freedom of choice. True relationship demands freedom to choose. We need to imitate God by giving people freedom to choose.

2. Freedom of religion is based on the doctrine of the image of God.

    As I mentioned previously, every person in our global community is created in God's image (Gen 1:26–28). When we look at someone, we shouldn't see them primarily through the lens of religion or race. We shouldn't see Buddhist, black, white, WASP (White, Anglo-Saxon

---

1. Heideman, "The Missiological Significance."

Protestant), Muslim, or Mexican. We should see God's image bearers. And when we see that image in others, when we treat people with dignity and equality, we honor God. Thus to coerce an image bearer against her will is an affront to her humanity. In fact, lack of religious freedom is an attack on God's image bearers.

3. Freedom of religion is based on the life of Christ.

    Jesus repeatedly called people to follow him. But he gave people freedom to choose. Some followed him and others didn't. In one of the most poignant moments in the gospels, it says that Jesus felt love for the rich young ruler who decided he would not follow Jesus (Mark 10:21). Jesus demonstrated a love that gave people freedom to accept or reject him. We need to imitate Jesus by giving people freedom to choose.

4. Freedom of religion is based on the Golden Rule.

    Jesus said, "In everything do to others as you would have them do to you; for this is the law and the prophets" (Matt 7:12). Surely everyone wants freedom to follow their conscience without coercion. I sure do! We must grant to everyone the same thing that we desire. We need to obey this command which summarizes the ethical demands of the Law and the Prophets.

5. Freedom of religion is based on the love command.

    Jesus said one of the greatest commands is to "love your neighbor as yourself" (Mark 12:31). The standard for love in this command is the phrase "as yourself." In other words, love means that I treat my neighbors just how I want to be treated. I want the freedom and protection to worship. This then is what I would want for my neighbor.

6. Freedom of religion is based on justice.

    The Old Testament frequently defines justice in terms of protecting the rights of the poor and needy.

    - "Give justice to the poor and the orphan; uphold the rights of the oppressed and the destitute" (Ps 82:3, NLT)
    - "Learn to do good. Seek justice. Help the oppressed. Defend the cause of orphans. Fight for the rights of widows" (Isa 1:17, NLT)

- "They deprive the poor of justice and deny the rights of the needy among my people. They prey on widows and take advantage of orphans" (Isa 10:2, NLT).

In other words, "God's justice aims at creating an egalitarian community in which all classes of people maintain their basic human rights," including the right to freedom of religion.[2]

People usually love talking about freedom of religion so long as you are talking about their religion. Yet a commitment to religious freedom is not a cover for promoting or privileging any one religion. Christians speak out against persecution of Christians, but few also speak out against the persecution of other faiths. Muslims speak out against Islamophobia, but few also speak out against persecution of Christians in Muslim countries. This focus on one's own faith community alone lacks ethical consistency and integrity. Religious freedom is not about "just us," it's about justice! Therefore we promote and protect it for all.

In 2008 I led a conference in Kenya of fifty evangelical leaders from around the world. One of the issues on the table was how to counter the increasing alienation between Muslims and Christians. I began the session with a presentation about my experience in the Common Word Dialogue at Yale—one of the highest profile dialogues between Christians and Muslims in modern times.

Many rejoiced to hear of the positive and robust dialogue that took place, and especially that evangelical leaders engaged in this dialogue without compromising the gospel.

One of the negative results of the Common Word Dialogue was that evangelicals were divided over how to respond. A large number (including myself) were positive about the Common Word, while a vocal minority was negative. There were many evangelicals caught in between, sympathetic to the dialogue, but not feeling like they could sign the Yale response because they disagreed with a few important phrases.

So we faced two crucial issues at Kenya: (1) increasing alienation between Muslims and Christians and (2) growing tension and division between evangelicals about how to respond to Muslims. In response to this, we wrote a consensus document for evangelicals called "The Grace and Truth Affirmation." This later grew into my book, *Grace and Truth: Toward Christlike Relationships with Muslims.*

---

2. Mafico, "Just, Justice."

Part IV: A Core Dream Worth Suffering For

In this document, we commend nine biblical guidelines for Christlike relations with Muslims, one of which is to be persistent in our call for religious freedom. Note that this statement affirms both the right to conversion along with the responsibility of ethical witness:

> We affirm the right of religious freedom for every person and community. We defend the right of Muslims to express their faith respectfully among Christians and of Christians to express their faith respectfully among Muslims. Moreover we affirm the right of Muslims and Christians alike to change religious beliefs, practices and/or affiliations according to their conscience. Thus we stand against all forms of religious persecution toward Muslims, Christians, or anyone else. God desires all people to make faith choices based on conscience and conviction rather than any form of coercion or violence (2 Corinthians 4:2).[3]

This kind of emphasis on human rights puts some evangelicals on edge. I can imagine someone asking, "As evangelicals we don't want to oppress other religions, but shouldn't we favor the Christian faith? Isn't that better for us, especially since Christianity is the truth?" In the US this kind of thinking is often linked to the view that America was once a Christian nation. ("It's time to take back our country for God!")

These are worthy questions and understandable convictions—deserving a serious response.

But let's be honest. It is impossible to argue that America was ever a Christian nation. Our Founding Fathers were definitely religious and included true followers of Christ. It *is* valid to say that Christianity was the majority religion when our country was founded, but we were never a Christian nation. The famous First Amendment to the Constitution makes this clear: "Congress shall make no law respecting an establishment of religion, or prohibiting the free exercise thereof."

This "establishment clause" was intended to eliminate the possibility of a state church (like the Church of England—from which some of our forefathers fled). The "free exercise clause" was intended to preserve the right of citizens to believe "according to the dictates of their own conscience."

A story about Benjamin Franklin illustrates what this meant to the Founding Fathers in practice. When churches closed their doors to the famous evangelist George Whitefield, Franklin built a new hall where he could speak. But this was not just for Christians. It was for the use of all

---

3. "Grace and Truth."

religions. Franklin boasted, "even if the Mufti of Constantinople were to send a missionary to preach Mahometanism to us, he would find a pulpit at his service."[4] For Benjamin Franklin the First Amendment meant there was a place in America for both the leading American evangelical and the Muslim Mufti of Constantinople!

This emphasis on religious liberty provides four important benefits. First, it resists political coercion. We don't want our government dictating or unduly influencing our faith commitments and practices. Our faith is between us and God. Second, it allows for a healthy expression of diversity. Our Lady of Liberty says, "Give me your tired, your poor, your huddled masses yearning to breathe free."

An invitation like that attracts a smorgasbord of peoples. Third, it allows for open-minded investigation of thought. It frees up people to examine, explore and consider alternatives. The gospel is in the marketplace of ideas. Fourth, it keeps our faith pure. Pressuring people to accept the gospel does not produce true disciples. Freedom of religion allows people to make choices out of their own free will, which leads to authentic Jesus followers.

I agree with Steven Waldman's studied assessment: "The Founding Faith, then, was not Christianity, and it was not secularism. It was religious liberty—a revolutionary formula for promoting faith by leaving it alone."[5] Jesus does fine in an environment where there is freedom of religion!

But is this emphasis on freedom of religion part of our mandate? Are we getting off track to be concerned about this ethical issue? I don't think so. The Evangelical Manifesto, signed by a veritable "who's who" of evangelicals gives wholehearted support to this cause:

> Let it be known unequivocally that we are committed to religious liberty for people of all faiths, including the right to convert to or from the Christian faith. We are firmly opposed to the imposition of theocracy on our pluralistic society.... We are also concerned about the illiberalism of politically correct attacks on evangelism. We have no desire to coerce anyone or to impose on anyone beliefs and behavior that we have not persuaded them to adopt freely, and that we do not demonstrate in our own lives, above all by love.... Thus every right we assert for ourselves is at once a right we defend for others. A right for a Christian is a right for a Jew, and a right for a secularist, and a right for a Mormon, and right for a Muslim,

---

4. Quoted in Waldman, *Founding Faith*, 30.
5. Ibid., xvi.

and a right for a Scientologist, and right for all the believers in all the faiths across this wide land.[6]

Freedom of religion is not just a pious devotional thought or a sentimental ideal to consider. It has positive and powerful implications in the real world. Brian Grimm's research led him to this startling conclusion:

> Our research on 143 countries finds that when governments and religious groups in society do not erect barriers to religious competition but respect and protect such activities as conversion and proselytism, religious violence is less. . . . In sum, religious freedom promotes stability, helps to consolidate democracy, and lessens religious violence.[7]

Freedom of choice is given to us by God and we expect it from others. Therefore, promoting and protecting freedom of religion for everyone is part of what it means to bless the nations. As Joshua Daneshforooz wisely affirms: "Promoting religious freedom for all people must be an essential part of Christian mission in the twenty-first century."[8]

---

6. "An Evangelical Manifesto."
7. Quoted in Roberts Jr., *Real-Time Connections*, 191.
8. Daneshforooz, *Loving Our Religious Neighbors*, 64.

11

Blessing and Peacemaking

If possible, so far as it depends on you, live at peace with everyone.

ROMANS 12:18

I attended a conference at the Naval War College in Rhode Island on "Religion and Security in World Affairs" (May 7–8, 2014). I loved the lectures and the lively interaction. Yet something deeper was being stirred in me. I couldn't pinpoint what it was until I recalled Martin Luther King, Jr.'s statement: "Those who love peace must learn to organize as effectively as those who love war."[1]

Oh how I wish followers of Jesus were as organized for the sake of peace as the US military is for the sake of war! In his commentary on Ephesians, Klyne Snodgrass suggests a practical way Jesus' followers can organize for peace:

> The church is a peace institute. . . . Numerous schools for war exist, and both amateurs and scholars study wars. Few people study peace. The church should be a place where people study and practice peace.[2]

---

1. McGee, "Five Ways."
2. *NIV Application Commentary, New Testament: Ephesians*, 153–54.

Part IV: A Core Dream Worth Suffering For

I don't know how many pastors and Christian leaders think the church should be a peace institute, but most believe that peacemaking should play some significant role in the church. As I will argue, peacemaking is the mission of God. Thus, it is an important part of what it means to bless the nations. Peacemaking *is* the way of the Lord and is a crucial part of what it means to pursue justice and righteousness (Gen 18:19).

My friend Pastor Steve Norman did a survey about peacemaking for his doctoral studies. Here's what he found:

> I recently conducted a research project that collected data from 15 pastors in personal interviews and 297 pastors through an online survey. Their feedback on this issue was almost unanimous:
>
> "Yes, I affirm the theory of peacemaking as a biblical value."
>
> "No, it's not something our church is currently doing."
>
> "Honestly, we'd have no idea where to start if we wanted to."[3]

Obviously there seems to be a gap between what pastors say they believe and what they actually practice when it comes to peacemaking. This gap was evident in my own beliefs and practices a decade ago. But now I see that Jesus is on a peace mission and has a comprehensive peace plan which can be summarized in three tasks.

1. *Live at peace with everyone.* If I had to choose only one verse in the entire Bible to summarize what Jesus expects of peacemakers, it would be Romans 12:18. This verse is a virtual one-verse peacemaking manual. Because it is both concise and comprehensive, I like to call it "Peacemaking for Dummies": "If it is possible, so far as it depends on you, live peaceably with all" (See also Heb 12:14).

   Notice how realistic Paul was about peacemaking. The condition, "If it is possible" acknowledges that it is not always possible to make peace. Even our most sincere efforts may fail. Peacemakers aren't always peace achievers.

   This verse also affirms proactive peacemaking: "If it is possible, *so far as it depends on you,* live peaceably with all." Since it involves at least two parties, reconciliation isn't always possible. But the responsibility for taking steps toward peace always rests on us as individuals. "So far as it depends on you!" We can't ignore it, and we can't wait for

---

3. Norman, "Pastors and the Peacemaking Paradox."

Blessing and Peacemaking

the other party to come to us. We are repeatedly commanded to take the initiative in pursuing peace ourselves.

Finally, notice the last phrase of Romans 12:18: "If it is possible, so far as it depends on you, *live peaceably with all.*" The Bible teaches peacemaking without borders. The scope of peacemaking is comprehensive. God expects us to pursue peace with family, friends, neighbors, atheists, Muslims, undocumented immigrants, gays, Democrats, and Republicans. No borders. No boundaries. No exceptions.

2. *Seek the peace of the city.* Jeremiah's exhortation to the Jews in Babylon provides a riveting description of peacemaking in an urban world: "But seek the welfare of the city where I have sent you into exile, and pray to the LORD on its behalf, for in its welfare you will find your welfare" (Jer 29:7).

The term *welfare* in this passage is a translation of the Hebrew term *shalom*. This one word is usually translated as peace, but also as prosperity, success, well-being, safety, welfare, health, deliverance, salvation, and completeness. In other words, *shalom* is turbo-charged peace, full-spectrum peace, peace amplified. It is multi-dimensional and comprehensive.

Jeremiah's great command portrays a vision for human flourishing—for all.

In New Testament terms, God was calling them to be salt and light, to glorify God through their loving deeds of service to those outside of the faith (Matt 5:13–16). God was urging them to "always seek after that which is good for one another and for all people" (1 Thess 5:15, NASB). What a profound paradigm for ministry in the urban world of the twenty-first century!

Imagine the impact of Jeremiah's exhortation on these Jewish exiles. Babylon was the evil empire. Babylonians were the enemies—their captors and oppressors. Psalm 137:8–9 gives us a snapshot of the seething hatred of the Jews toward the Babylonians, "O Babylon, you will be destroyed. Happy is the one who pays you back for what you have done to us. Happy is the one who takes your babies and smashes them against the rocks" (NLT).

Yet God commands these Jewish exiles to seek the peace of Babylon. Basically God was telling them to love their enemies, the very ones who had so cruelly oppressed them. This was astounding. No one in recorded history had ever said anything like this before—until

Jesus came on the scene six centuries later: "Love your enemies and pray for those who persecute you, so that you may be children of your Father in heaven" (Matt 5:44–45).

What does it mean practically to seek the peace of the city? It is a call to pursue justice, to seek racial reconciliation, to strive for harmony between different religious communities, to work to alleviate poverty and to care for creation. Shalom is another way of talking about blessing.

To have the greatest impact, we need to do this in partnership with those outside the church. The basis of shalom-producing partnerships outside of the church centers around three terms. We need to learn about common grace, common ground, and the common good. These terms were not even part of my vocabulary for the first thirty-five years of my walk with Jesus. But as God led me into peacemaking my eyes were opened.

Common grace teaches that God's grace overflows to every creature on earth. God has given humanity four gifts:

- All people enjoy the blessings of the physical world.
- All people have the ability to do good (implying restraint of evil as well).
- All people have a general knowledge of God or a sense of the divine.
- All people are culture makers.

By common grace, unbelievers do good; in fact, they often do amazing things. We should see God's hand in it. We should be grateful that God's common grace operates in every friendship, every act of kindness, every scientific discovery, and every technological advance. For all of this is ultimately from God.

Because of common grace, we have common ground with unbelievers. We have a basis to work in partnership with the government, businesses, nonprofit organizations, people of different faiths, or those with no faith at all. There are *many* areas where we can work together. We can cooperate without compromise. The goal of partnering is the common good, which is another way of talking about shalom or human flourishing.

Seeking the shalom of the city in this way pleases God and multiplies our impact. It also enhances our witness. Good deeds lead to goodwill, which opens the door for the good news.

3. *Believe and share the gospel of peace.* The gospel is described in terms of peace five times in the New Testament,[4] indicating the close relationship between the gospel and peacemaking.

The gospel of peace was first preached to a man of war—Cornelius the Centurion! God supernaturally led the apostle Peter to the home of the Roman Centurion, Cornelius (Acts 10). Cornelius was just the kind of person Peter didn't want to share with. Cornelius was a Gentile; he lived in the wrong place—Caesarea (the Roman capital of the province of Judea), and he was the enemy, an occupying soldier. These are some of the reasons it took three God-inspired visions before Peter was willing to meet with Cornelius.

What was Peter's message? "You know the message God sent to the people of Israel, announcing *the good news of peace* through Jesus Christ, who is Lord of all" (Acts 10:36, NIV, emphasis mine). This Gentile man of war believed the gospel of peace and experienced both reconciliation with God and with his Jewish neighbor Peter.

It is important to note that peace is at the heart of the gospel even when the word *peace* is not explicitly used to describe it. An understanding of Jesus' person, teaching, example, death, resurrection, and return highlight the prominence of peace in the gospel. For the sake of brevity I will only give a few illustrations.

Three times in the Bible Jesus' very person is described as peace. In Isaiah he is called the Prince of Peace (Isaiah 9:6); in Micah he is the coming ruler from Bethlehem who "will be our peace" (Mic 5:2–5, NIV); and in Ephesians Paul says Jesus "himself is our peace" (Eph 2:13–14, NIV).

Jesus' teaching also highlights peacemaking, especially in the Sermon on the Mount:

- "Blessed are the peacemakers, for they will be called children of God" (Matt 5:9).
- "Be reconciled" (Matt 5:24).
- "Forgive those who sin against you" (Matt 6:12, 14–15; Luke 17:3–4).

4. Acts 10:24–43; Rom 5:1; Eph 2:13–17, 6:15; Col 1:19–20.

- "Do not judge so that you may not be judged. . . . first take the log out of your own eye, and then you will see clearly to take the speck out of your neighbor's eye" (Matt 7:1, 5).
- "Love your enemies" (Matt 5:44).

Jesus' death on the cross procures peace for his people and all creation (Col 1:20; Eph 2:13–17). And finally his second coming portrays peace as the end game of history. Swords will be hammered into plowshares and spears into pruning hooks, and war will cease (Mic 4:3–4). The wolf will live with the lamb, the leopard will lie down with the goat, the calf and the lion and the yearling together (Isa 11:6–9). The future messiah will make an everlasting covenant of peace (Ezek 37:24–27) that will usher in perfect social, political, and ecological peace.

Thus the good news affirms this profound reality: Jesus has waged decisive peace in the world. The kingdom of peace has been inaugurated. The future of peace is assured. But we don't just wait for the future. We begin implementing Jesus' comprehensive peace plan now "on earth as it is in heaven" (Matt 6:10).

We seek to live at peace with everyone; we seek the peace of the city; we believe and share the gospel of peace. If we take these three tasks seriously, we just may become the "peace institute" the church is called to be. Peacemaking is the mission of God and an important part of what it means to bless the nations!

12

Blessing and Sharing the Gospel with Integrity
The Ethics of Evangelism

> Mission belongs to the very being of the church. Proclaiming the word of God and witnessing to the world is essential for every Christian. At the same time, it is necessary to do so according to gospel principles, with full respect and love for all human beings.
>
> CHRISTIAN WITNESS IN A MULTI-RELIGIOUS WORLD
> WORLD COUNCIL OF CHURCHES
> PONTIFICAL COUNCIL FOR INTERRELIGIOUS DIALOGUE
> WORLD EVANGELICAL ALLIANCE

Robert Seiple, first-ever US Ambassador-at-Large for International Religious Freedom, knows a lot about the persecution Christians face around the world. He knows the realities of suffering our sisters and brothers in the global church endure. But he also knows that some persecution and conflict is brought about because of unwise and misguided approaches to witnessing . . . like this:

Part IV: A Core Dream Worth Suffering For

In 1998 thirty Filipino Christians were put in jail for distributing Bibles in Saudi Arabia. When Seiple visited the Philippine Embassy in Saudi a few months after the event the Ambassador told him, "under Saudi Arabian law you can bring one Bible in the country in your briefcase." These people tried to smuggle 20,000 of them into the country. Then they claimed Saudi Arabia for Christ by the year 2000! . . . They were running out of time . . . and here they still had all these Bibles. So they started to walk down the streets of Riyadh, throwing Bibles over the walls, literally hitting unsuspecting Muslims on the head. Saudi Arabia's *Muttawa* (religious police) stepped in immediately . . . and 30 of my countrymen ended up in jail.[1]

Not the greatest approach to witness . . . "Bible bombardment!" An extreme example? Yes, but no one can deny that there have been vast numbers of well-meaning but wisdom-lacking approaches to witnessing around the world. I appreciate the zeal of my Filipino brothers but I wholeheartedly disagree with their method. Bad methods almost always undermine a good message and sincere motives.

I want all people, including Muslims, to follow Jesus. Some of the Muslims whom I am privileged to know through my work may experience life-transforming encounters with Jesus. I welcome this and recognize that some of these may choose to live out the implications of that as Muslims within the Muslim community, while others may choose to change their religious affiliation. I am committed to defending their fundamental human right to make that decision for themselves, and I will give them as much or as little help as they want in thinking through how to live out their discipleship. In the same way, there may be evangelicals who, in the course of my work, feel led to become Muslims. While I would naturally try to persuade them against this, ultimately I must in the same way support their following their own convictions.

I deeply appreciate Sheikh Habib Ali Al-Jifri's perspective. During the Common Word Dialogue at Yale, we had a closed-door session to discuss the issue of *da'wa* (Islamic outreach) and evangelism. Twenty-eight high-level Muslim and Christian leaders engaged in a lively and at times emotionally charged dialogue. Near the end of our time, Sheikh Al-Jifri concluded: "I do not have any problem with evangelicals sharing their faith anywhere, because I am convinced about my faith."

---

1. Seiple, "From Bible Bombardment to Incarnational Evangelism," 29.

I feel the same way! As an evangelical, I believe that God is sovereign and all-powerful. I believe that Jesus and the Holy Spirit are actively working in people's hearts, so I can relax. All I need to do is follow Jesus, speak of Jesus, and leave the results to him.

Nevertheless, *da'wa* and evangelism remain an area of tension, suspicion, and conflict between Muslims and Christians. Both Christianity and Islam are missionary faiths. Large numbers of Christians convert to Islam on a regular basis, and large numbers of Muslims become followers of Jesus on a regular basis. How can both Muslims and Christians respectfully bear witness to their faith and yet live in peace?

Here's what I think we need to do from the Christian side of this challenge. Evangelism is a non-negotiable pillar of evangelical faith. Jesus commands us to bear witness to our faith (Matt 28:18–20; Acts 1:8), so the real issue is not *whether* we witness but *how* we witness.

Jesus, Peter, and Paul all emphasize the importance of how we witness:

- See, I am sending you out like sheep into the midst of wolves; so be wise as serpents and innocent as doves (Matt 10:16).

- But in your hearts sanctify Christ as Lord. Always be ready to make your defense to anyone who demands from you an accounting for the hope that is in you (1 Pet 3:15).

- Conduct yourselves wisely toward outsiders, making the most of the time. Let your speech always be gracious, seasoned with salt, so that you may know how you ought to answer everyone (Col 4:5–6).

We are called to be both shrewd and innocent in our outreach. We answer people's questions about our faith—which assumes we have a relationship with them. And we communicate our faith with gentleness and respect, wisdom and grace.

I am painfully aware that evangelical practice sometimes fails in this respect. There are evangelicals who use relief and development as a cover and do "aid evangelism" (aid as a means to evangelism). For example, there are some groups who demand that unbelievers hear the Lord's message before they receive the Lord's medicine. They seek to be as "shrewd as snakes" but they fail to be as "innocent as doves." Using inducements to convert others is unethical.

Relief and development should be provided as an act of love, without any strings attached. That's what Jesus did. He never demanded that people listen to him before he would heal them.

Part IV: A Core Dream Worth Suffering For

This does not mean, however, that we can't share our faith as relief and development workers. It means that the best way of sharing our faith is in response to questions people have. We share the gospel with integrity when we follow the teaching of Peter, "give an *answer* to everyone who asks you" (1 Pet 3:15, NIV, emphasis mine) and Paul "so that you may know how you ought to *answer* everyone" (Col 4:6, emphasis mine).

My good friend Bob Roberts Jr. used this approach in Afghanistan. When he met with a government official he made this promise:

> My name is Bob Roberts and we are here to serve and help your people if you want us. I am a pastor of a church in America but I am here to serve you and will respect your laws. I won't preach or pass out tracts or do "missionary" work, but if people ask me about my faith I will answer their questions. The people who come will do the same. We will not disobey your laws, but we will not hide the fact that we are Christians.
>
> We will build the schools. In the meantime you read the New Testament and we will read the Qur'an—to get to know each other's faith better.[2]

Perhaps the best way to illustrate ethical evangelism, that is, sharing the gospel with integrity, is to apply the Golden Rule to our witness—"In everything do to others as you would have them do to you; for this is the law and the prophets" (Matt 7:12). Does the Golden Rule guide our outreach? Imagine a religion or cult with whom you disagree or even adamantly oppose. Is it Mormonism? Scientology? Jehovah's Witnesses? The Church of Satan? The Ku Klux Klan? Islam? Hinduism? Now picture them witnessing about their faith, using the same methods that you use to witness to others. How would you feel about that?

I remember years ago witnessing to high school students. I would walk on campus after school was out with a close friend. As adults, there was a power imbalance between us and the students. Afterward, the wife of my friend told us that it was wrong to witness to young people like this because of the power imbalance. I didn't see it at the time. But if adults of any religion or cult went on campus to witness to my children, I now realize that I would not like it!

Many people understand evangelism and proselytism as referring to the same thing. But I think it is wise to distinguish between the two. Proselytism is normally used in a pejorative sense, implying forcing one's faith

---

2. Roberts Jr., *Glocalization*, 109.

on another—unworthy witness. By contrast, evangelism refers to a positive presentation of the good news of Jesus. It does not attack other faiths or perspectives but bears witness to Jesus. Evangelism usually involves dialogue and sometimes includes persuasive rational argument.

Proselytism or unworthy witness happens primarily in three ways:

1. When one's *motives* are wrong (seeing people as projects, befriending people only to witness to them, being preoccupied with success in the eyes of one's donors or organization).

2. When one's *methods* are inconsistent with the gospel (when we do not treat the people we witness to as God's image bearers, worthy of dignity; when we break the Golden Rule in our witness and do not treat them how we would want to be treated; when we have hidden agendas or hidden identities; when we use coercion, deception or financial inducement to compel people to convert).

3. When one's *message* is wrong (when we attack the faith of another rather than speaking of Jesus; when we misrepresent the other's faith—bearing false witness—to get them to convert to ours).

Precisely because Christians have sometimes been rightly accused of unworthy witness, *The Cape Town Commitment* confesses: "We commit ourselves to be scrupulously ethical in all our evangelism. Our witness is to be marked by 'gentleness and respect, keeping a clear conscience.' We therefore reject any form of witness that is coercive, unethical, deceptive, or disrespectful."

Bearing witness graciously, gently, or respectfully isn't always the norm among evangelicals. But happily there are a large number of evangelicals who seek to share their faith in a manner worthy of Jesus.

In a joint statement entitled *Why Do We Share the Good News about Jesus with All Peoples, Including Muslims?* leaders of fifty-five Christian organizations from nineteen countries affirm the importance of respectful witness and specifically reject what has historically been referred to as "aid evangelism": "We, who come from many cultures, countries and backgrounds, offer this message of peace to all people in love, with respect and cultural sensitivity, without coercion or material inducement" (Affirmation 5).[3]

---

3. *Rick Love* website, "Why do we Share the Good News About Jesus with all Peoples, Including Muslims?"

Part IV: A Core Dream Worth Suffering For

A far more important, historic, groundbreaking declaration on the ethics of witness was hammered out between liberal Protestants, Roman Catholics, and evangelicals in 2011. Over a five-year period, the Pontifical Council for Interreligious Dialogue (PCID), the World Council of Churches (WCC), and the World Evangelical Alliance (WEA) produced a document called *Christian Witness in a Multi-Religious World: Recommendations for Conduct*.[4]

The preamble begins with a robust affirmation: "Mission belongs to the very being of the church. Proclaiming the word of God and witnessing to the world is essential for every Christian." It then rightly continues, "At the same time, it is necessary to do so according to gospel principles, with full respect and love for all human beings."

This document included input from evangelicals but it doesn't read like a typical evangelical document. It does, however, outline excellent recommendations for ethical evangelism. We need to encourage followers of Jesus around the world to engage with this document and apply its precepts.

As mentioned previously, one of the best ways to share the gospel with greater integrity is to become incarnational in our witness. Eugene Peterson's well-known paraphrase, *The Message*, puts it compellingly: "The Word became flesh and blood, and moved into the neighborhood" (John 1:14). We are commanded to imitate the humility and sacrificial nature of Jesus in the incarnation. Not only does Paul say this, but Jesus himself commissions us in the same way: "As the Father has sent me, so I send you" (John 20:21). This is the broadest mandate of all the Great Commission passages in the New Testament. Like Jesus, we are sent to speak of the kingdom of God. Like Jesus, we are sent to demonstrate the kingdom by feeding the hungry, healing the sick, and loving the marginalized. We are called to represent Jesus' real presence in a wounded, weary world.

The incarnation speaks of presence and proximity. People will see our lives—warts and all. But hopefully they will catch a glimpse of "Christ in [us], the hope of glory" as well (Col 1:27).

To be incarnational is to follow the one who is a friend of "sinners." Jesus hung out with the wrong crowd. He embraced the marginalized, the moral misfits, and the nonreligious. Jesus got a bad reputation because he partied with people: "The Son of Man has come eating and drinking, and you say, 'Look, a glutton and a drunkard, a friend of tax collectors and sinners!'" (Luke 7:34).

---

4. *World Evangelicals* website, "Christian Witness in a Multi-Religious World."

Jesus embodied the welcoming grace of God. He engaged all types of people but never compromised his integrity. He taught and modeled both *exclusive truth claims* ("I am the way, the truth, and the life. No one comes to the Father except through me" [John 14:6]) and *inclusive love aims* ("Love your neighbor as yourself"[Mark 12:31] and "Love your enemies" [Matt 5:44]). So should we.

PART V

Bearers of Blessing Among Neighbors and Nations

13

Aligning Ourselves with a Glocal World

> The seven last words of a dying church:
> "We've never done it this way before!"
>
> AUTHOR UNKNOWN

I was talking to a pastor named Jack about what it means to follow Jesus in a glocalized world. He totally got it and then exclaimed, "This will involve a radical re-education of the church!" Yes it will. New paradigms demand profound shifts. Following Jesus among our neighbors and among the nations in a glocalized world demands change in at least four areas. We need to:

1. Review and revise all public communication.
2. Focus on integrity, humility, and identity.
3. Train workers and churches in "glocal" ministry.
4. Adapt our organizations to twenty-first-century realities.

Part V: Bearers of Blessing Among Neighbors and Nations

REVIEW AND REVISE ALL PUBLIC COMMUNICATION

We need to examine all vehicles of communication (especially our websites) to make sure the content, spirit, and terms used communicate most effectively to all audiences. To help me with this, I often imagine a Muslim and a secular person looking over my shoulder when I write or sitting in the audience when I speak. The use of once-cherished terms like *Christian, missions, missionary,* and *church planting* have become stumbling blocks in many contexts, carrying unintended negative meanings. As a result, in our attempts to bring blessing to the nations, we are too easily misunderstood. Sometimes, a change in terminology involves some re-theologizing. For example, our cherished term for ourselves—*Christian*—is actually only used three times in the New Testament. On the other hand, the term *disciple* is used more than 250 times. Which term communicates best? In many contexts, the term *disciple,* or the dynamic equivalent, *follower of Jesus,* is much more descriptive and relevant.

The term *missions* was first coined by Ignatius of Loyola in the 1500s.[1] Since then, despite the many good deeds of missionaries enhancing human flourishing around the globe, the term has come to imply aggressive proselytism and cultural imperialism, rather than respectful witness. Is there a biblical term or concept that better communicates what we mean by *missions*?

Word choice can make a profound difference in the way that our audiences receive our message, as well as the way we think about ourselves. Let me reiterate, however, that a change in our *being* is as important as a change in our *wording.* The goal is integrity and humility in our communication and in our person. Here are some possible changes of terminology that may help us communicate more effectively.

---

1. Bosch, *Transforming Mission,* 228.

Aligning Ourselves with a Glocal World

Old Terms	New Terms
Missions	blessing the nations, global engagement, God's global purposes, reconciliation, peacemaking
Missionary	international staff, ambassador, social entrepreneur, businessperson (aid worker, teacher, and so forth) living an intentional Christian life
Christian	follower of Jesus, disciple
Convert	follower of Jesus, disciple
church planting	Disciple making, gospel planting, forming communities of Jesus followers
mission agency	faith-based organization, apostolic community, religious order
Church	community of faith, community of Jesus followers, community of hope, community of reconciliation
church missions department	global engagement, global relations, international task force, international peacemaking and justice department, international reconciliation task force
non-Christians	non-Christians[A]
Field	adopted homeland, host country

A. Originally I had the terms like *God seeker, unbeliever,* and *pre-believer* but I realize that it is more respectful to define them as they define themselves (atheist, Muslim) or as non-Christians.

FOCUS ON INTEGRITY, HUMILITY, AND IDENTITY

Discerning an integrated identity is no easy task. We need to embrace a holistic approach to work and witness. We evaluate our skills, examine our passions, and assess our opportunities to find the work that best fits the way God has made us. In this way we align our motivation, our work, our personal gifting, and our calling to bring heaven to earth.

As a follower of Jesus, this integrated identity should also manifest integrity and humility. Integrity means that our message, methods, and motives are congruent. As Bob Roberts Jr. says, "Serve not to convert but because you have been converted. The motive of Jesus is serving others, not using the gospel as religious bait."[2]

As mentioned previously, incarnational ministry demands humility. Will we embrace this virtue spurned by many but exemplified in the life

2. Roberts Jr., *Glocalization*, 139.

of Christ? Jesus described himself as "gentle and humble of heart" (Matt 11:29) and pronounced a blessing on the meek (Matt 5:5). Jesus-centered, kingdom-focused people realize that "God is opposed to the proud but gives grace to the humble" (1 Pet 5:5).

Money, sex, and power are often described as the three big temptations we must overcome to be fruitful for the kingdom. The love of money has never been a temptation for me. Early on in my walk with Jesus, God convicted me and cleansed me from sexual impurity. And to this day I work hard at remaining pure. But I was addicted to power. And I had never heard a sermon about the dangers of pride or power. So humility wasn't part of my MO as a young leader, until God got a hold of me.

Over a two-week period, God shined the light of his holiness on the darkness of my pride and I was undone. I felt the ugliness of my pride in the depth of my being. I remember attending a Vineyard "Signs and Wonders Conference" at that time. Everyone was being blessed, joyfully sensing and seeing God's power. But I just wept over my sin.

One of the leaders on my team said, "Rick, I am sorry that you are going through this. But I've gotta say, you are a lot easier to relate to since your repentance!" Yes, humble people are easy to get along with. Maybe that's because they are being like Jesus!

Blessing the nations in a glocalized world demands heartfelt repentance for many of us. I stepped down from my role as the international director of a large mission agency because I personally could no longer live out my faith with integrity in that role and within that ministry paradigm. While many people in traditional mission organizations or churches do not struggle with this like I do, there are thousands of people like me who feel restricted by this paradigm. They feel that this model of ministry potentially undermines their integrity, robs them of joy, and quenches their boldness. In fact, I believe God is raising up a whole new generation of people who will embrace a 3D approach to life and ministry:

- confessing Jesus as their core message worth dying for
- embodying an integrated identity worthy living for
- embracing the call to bless all nations as a global dream worth suffering for.

TRAIN WORKERS AND CHURCHES IN "GLOCAL" MINISTRY

Training workers like Paul the apostle—who have integrated identities, combining first-class work with fruitful disciple making—is *the* challenge of the twenty-first century. This is true whether they serve among their neighbors locally or in foreign countries. But we don't just want to train a select group of people, historically known as missionaries. We want to train everyone in our churches to model excellent work and effective disciple making. The glocal paradigm of ministry believes the whole church is sent into the world, not just a few missionaries. Because of this, we train whole congregations to incarnate the gospel in every vocation and location, on every day of the week.[3]

The church tends to exacerbate a sense of dual identity with their international staff since they embrace old missionary paradigms (and terms) and in practice only understand the role of the classic, fully-supported missionary. That worked in the eighteenth through twentieth centuries, but not in the twenty-first century! Likewise, Bible schools and theological seminaries have done little to train bi-vocational disciple makers with integrated identities because their focus has been on training those in pastoral work or full-time ministry. We need training models that are more holistic and relevant to following Jesus among our neighbors and among the nations in the work place.

ADAPT OUR ORGANIZATIONS TO TWENTY-FIRST-CENTURY REALITIES

A number of disciples serving in restricted-access countries have a well-established, integrated identity in their adopted homelands. They readily identify themselves as followers of Jesus who are living cross-culturally as businesspeople or in another role. However, when they return to their sending country, they face the dual-identity tension as they identify with their organization. As one brother told me, "Rick, I love my agency. But I am scared to death that one of my Muslim neighbors will find out that I am part of this agency!" It's time to end this duplicity and seek true integrity. It's time to change our organizations or start new ones that allow followers

---

3. As I mentioned previously, the glocal paradigm of ministry has much in common with the missional church movement.

Part V: Bearers of Blessing Among Neighbors and Nations

of Christ to walk in integrity and enjoy an integrated identity. It's time for some future-thinking church leaders to come up with new ways of thinking, communicating, and sending their members cross-culturally. One friend of mine commented,

> Right now, my sending church doesn't include me in their little "missionary booklet." But wouldn't it be amazing if that booklet were transformed and they had a catalog of "members who are part of our church family though God has moved them on to new places." ... It could include a variety of people: traditional missionaries, people who've moved overseas for business, etc.—not just those who receive financial support from the church, but those for whom the church has intentionally committed to actively pray and send out from their midst in a variety of roles. Just a dream ... I can even think of very real and pertinent prayer requests that could be publically displayed in my church that I would be proud to show to people in my adopted homeland.

I write this book to challenge the status quo and help followers of Jesus adjust to a glocal world. Having said that, I see a whole spectrum of ways people will try to apply this book to their personal lives and organizations (see below). If you have taken the time to read this book then you probably won't fit in the "ignorant or not concerned" category. Some will remain in the "missionary" category. A number of organizations will probably "adjust their websites and literature," seeking to be more careful about how they communicate in light of multiple audiences. A smaller category will seek to "birth sister organizations" that are glocal, with the hope that they will maintain an interdependent (or covenant) relationship with them. Finally, there will be innovators who will pioneer new organizations or radically rebrand old ones.

The 3D Spectrum

Ignorant or not concerned	Missionary visas and/or identity	Website and literature change	Birthing sister 3D organizations	Radical rebranding or new organizations

14

Starting a Glocal Reformation
Lessons Learned from Martin Luther

I have always been fascinated by Martin Luther, the great sixteenth-century Reformer. He was a profound thinker, a spiritual revolutionary, and a polarizing person prone to overstatement. He was a man of extremes. He struggled with depression and yet boldly confronted the failures of the church of his day. He seemed to have an opinion on everything. This passionate Reformer loved to theologize, and he liked to party. He would often have theological discussions over beer and good food.

How could one man have such a radical impact on the church and the world?

I wanted to answer that question, because like Luther, my goal is to instigate a reformation—a glocal reformation.

So a few years ago I went on a personal "Martin Luther tour" with my good friend Friedrich Leonhardt. It was nice having a German friend who could translate for me if I didn't understand something! Together we made this a spiritual pilgrimage.

We drove to most of the great Luther sites. Friedrich and I would take our time at each place pondering what happened. Then we would pray silently by ourselves. Next, we would debrief—sharing our thoughts and feelings and talking about what we sensed God was teaching us. We had a great time!

It was sobering to see the Wartburg Castle, where Luther translated the New Testament into German (instead of Latin), along with writing other works on doctrine. Luther called this his own "Patmos," seeing himself in exile like the Apostle John when he wrote the book of Revelation (Rev 1:9).

Being locked away for a year like this translating the New Testament must have been tortuous. This was one of the early attempts in modern history to do a dynamic equivalent translation. It was Luther's version of Eugene Peterson's famous *The Message*. His translation became a key tool for Luther's reformation of the church.

As I pondered and prayed about Luther, it got me thinking about my own captivity. I have been thinking about the challenges of following Jesus in a glocalized world for over a decade. I have worked out of my own home for the last ten years, seeking to live this out, struggling to put in writing some reflections on this crucial topic. But I realize that I needed this captivity because God had to do a lot of heart work in me. Humbling, but true.

We went to All Saints Church in Wittenberg where Luther nailed the Ninety-Five Theses to the church doors, sparking the Reformation. This event is usually portrayed as a defiant challenge to the Church by a prophet resisting the status quo. Luther supposedly threw down the gauntlet. We envision him boldly proclaiming: "My way or the highway!" But in fact he wasn't doing this. Luther was calling for dialogue about these issues. This was the normal procedure of the times.[1]

Like Luther, I write this book as a call for dialogue. I have tried to be carefully nuanced and to speak with love (and I am sure I have failed in many cases). But I am calling for change—even radical change. My prayer is that this book will challenge the way you see the world and your work in it. I hope it encourages you in your walk with Jesus and shakes up your paradigms of ministry. But I am no prophet. My spiritual vision is not "20/20." This book is merely a starting point for dialogue.

At one of Luther's sites, Friedrich and I looked over the many tracts, booklets, and books Luther wrote during the Reformation. Luther was prolific—a ministry machine!

The Gutenberg Press had revolutionized communication during Luther's age. For the first time in history, books could be printed in mass quantity rather than being copied by hand. And Luther capitalized on this new invention. He captured the social media of his era to foment change.

---

1. Hans Hillerbrand writes that Luther had no intention of confronting the church, but saw his disputation as a scholarly objection to church practices, and the tone of the writing is accordingly "searching, rather than doctrinaire." "Martin Luther," *Wikipedia*.

As I stood looking at this table full of literature, I received what I believe was a word from God. I needed to capture and capitalize on the social media of the day, if I was going to challenge the status quo and start a glocal reformation. Since then I have been active as a blogger; I am a friend of Facebook; and of course I tweet. But there is so much more work I need to do.

What is especially significant about this is that social media is both a huge reason there needs to be change, and one of the key means of bringing change. In fact I think I need to tweet that last comment and put it on Facebook!

Finally, we went to Worms, where Luther faced the general assembly of the Holy Roman Empire. This is where Luther stood on trial before the authorities about his writings. It is referred to as the Diet of Worms in history. (No, it doesn't refer to a bunch of fat guys needing to lose weight, although that might have been the case. *Diet* means "deliberative assembly.")

During our time of debriefing, Friedrich made an insightful comment. "Rick, did you notice the architecture of this place? Luther stood all alone facing these leaders who sat far above him in pomp and glory. The way it is built would be very intimidating." It would have been hard enough facing all these leaders alone. Doing so in this structure magnified the power of the Church. Luther must have felt like David facing Goliath.

This leads to my third and final big lesson from my Luther tour. Luther's response to the church establishment was firm but not dogmatic. He did not think he had it all together. He was not above correction. Here is what he said:

> Unless I am convinced by the testimony of the Scriptures or by clear reason (for I do not trust either in the pope or in councils alone, since it is well known that they have often erred and contradicted themselves), I am bound by the Scriptures I have quoted and my conscience is captive to the Word of God. I cannot and will not recant anything, since it is neither safe nor right to go against conscience. May God help me. Amen.[2]

His concluding words give me much encouragement. Luther had robust convictions based on Scripture, reason, and conscience. But note carefully, he was willing to change his convictions if someone could prove to him through Scripture or careful reasoning that he was wrong. If someone

---

2. Ibid.

could appeal to his conscience and help him see things in a new light, he would change.

I am no Luther, but I am passionate about the need for a reformation! I am a man convinced by Scripture and reason that the church needs a new ministry paradigm for the twenty-first century. So here I stand. I want to be bold, yet receptive to counsel. Where I am wrong, I ask that you show me through Scripture or reasoning. Appeal to my conscience. But if I have convinced you that I am right, I ask you to follow me and the growing company of others like me, as I follow Jesus in a glocalized world.

And here's what all this means in a few sound bites: following Jesus in a glocalized world is not about making our message acceptable to everyone or being politically correct. It's not about seeking greater security or avoiding persecution. It's not about watering down our global mandate, nor does it affirm a naïve transparency that lacks prudence.

Following Jesus in a glocalized world is about realizing the profound impact that terrorism, pluralism, and globalization have on the way we live, think, and minister. It's about adjusting to the communicational complexities of the twenty-first century. It's about having a holistic view of life, work, and ministry. It's about having personal and organizational integrity. It's about embracing God's plan to bless all nations as our global dream. It's about being incarnational. It's about embodying and sharing the good news of Jesus.

Works Cited

2008 Conference. 2008. faith.yale.edu/common-word/2008-conference.
Barnett, P. W. "Tentmaking." In *Dictionary of Paul and His Letters (electronic edition),* edited by G. F. Hawthorne, R. P. Martin, and D. G. Reid, 926–27. Downers Grove, IL: InterVarsity, 1993.
Bauckham, Richard. *Bible and Mission: Christian Witness in a Postmodern World.* Grand Rapids: Baker, 2005.
Bill of Rights. Accessed January 18, 2015. www.archives.gov/exhibits/charters/bill_of_ rights_transcript.html#text.
Blomberg, Craig. *Application Commentary, New Testament: 1 Corinthians.* Grand Rapids: Zondervan, 1994.
Borelli, John. "Christian-Muslim Relations in the United States." *The Muslim World* 84 (July 2004) 321–33.
Bosch, David J. *Transforming Mission: Paradigm Shifts in Theology of Mission.* New York: Orbis, 1993.
Boyd, Gregory. *The Myth of a Christian Nation.* Grand Rapids: Zondervan, 2005.
Breslin, Scott. "The Workplace Priest: Activating our God-Given Identity as Priests at Work." *Evangelical Missions Quarterly* (2015) 286–95.
Brinkhoff, Thomas. *The Principal Agglomerations of the World.* January 1, 2015. https:// www.frontiermissionfellowship.org/uploads/documents/Four%20Men%20 Three%20Eras.pdf.
Bruce, F. F. *Commentary on the Book of Acts.* Grand Rapids: Eerdmans, 1975.
Carson, D. A. "Matthew/Exposition of Matthew/II. The Gospel of the Kingdom (3:17:29)/B. First Discourse: The Sermon on the Mount (5:1—7:29)/6. Balance and perfection (7:1–12)/b. The danger of being undiscerning (7:6)." *The Expositor's Bible Commentary: Pradis CD-ROM.* Book Version 4.0.2.
"Christian Witness in a Multi-Religious World." January 25–28, 2011. http://www. worldevangelicals.org/pdf/1106Christian_Witness_in_a_Multi-Religious_World. pdf.
"Colossians/V. Appeal for Christian Living (3:1–4:6)/B. Guidelines for the Christian Life (3:5–4:6)/4. Religious duties to be faithfully performed (4:2–6)/b. The duty of witnessing (4:5, 6)." *The Expositor's Bible Commentary: Pradis CD-ROM: Colossians.* Version 4.0.2.
A Common Word. October 13, 2007. www.acommonword.com.
Consultation on Mission Language and Metaphors. "Biblical Language and Military Metaphors: Sticks and stones revisited." *http://ricklove.net/wp-content/*

Works Cited

uploads/2010/04/Biblical-Language-and-Military-Metaphors-web-copy.pdf. October, 2000. Accessed February 18, 2011. http://ricklove.net/wp-content/uploads/2010/04/Biblical-Language-and-Military-Metaphors-web-copy.pdf.

Crewdson, John. "Internet Blows CIA Cover; It's Easy to Track America's Covert Operatives. All you Need to Know is How to Navigate the Internet." *The Chicago Tribune*, March 12, 2006.

Daneshforooz, Joshua W. *Loving Our Religious Neighbors*. Self-published, 2011.

DuBose, Francis M. *God Who Sends*. Nashville: Broadman, 1983.

Eck, Diana L. *A New Religious America: How a "Christian Country" Has Become the World's Most Religiously Diverse Nation*. San Francisco: HarperSanFrancisco, 1997.

"Economic Development." *The City of San Diego*. March 1, 2011. Accessed January 10, 2015. http://www.sandiego.gov/economic-development/sandiego/population.shtml.

"An Evangelical Manifesto." 2008. http://www.anevangelicalmanifesto.com/docs/Evangelical_Manifesto.pdf.

Everts, J. M. "Financial Support." In *Dictionary of Paul and His Letters*, 295–99, electronic edition. Downers Grove, IL: InterVarsity, 1993.

Fee, Gordon. *The First Epistle to the Corinthians: The New International Commentary on the New Testament*. Grand Rapids: Eerdmans, 1987.

France, R. T. *The Gospel of Matthew*. Grand Rapids: Eerdmans, 2007.

Friedman, Thomas. "Thomas Friedman Remarks to U.S. Conference of Mayors." January 19, 2012. www.c-span.org/video/?303778-2thomas-friedman-remarks-us-conference-mayors.

———. *The World is Flat: A Brief History of the Twenty-First Century*. New York: Farrar, Straus and Giroux, 2005.

Galli, Mark. "Putting Evangelism on Hold." *Christianity Today*. November 16, 2010. Accessed February 18, 2011. http://www.christianitytoday.com/ct/2010/novemberweb-only/55-21.0.html?start=1.

Garland, David E. "Being Wise in Reaching Outsiders (4:5–6)." In *NIV Application Commentary, New Testament: Colossians and Philemon*, 272. Electronic edition. Grand Rapids: Zondervan, 1998.

Ghobari, Mohammed. "Response to 'proselytizing'? Al Qaeda Group Claims Killing of US Teacher in Yemen." *The Christian Science Monitor*. March 18, 2012. Accessed January 10, 2015. http://www.csmonitor.com/World/Latest-News-Wires/2012/0318/Response-to-proselytizing-Al-Qaeda-group-claims-killing-of-US-teacher-in-Yemen.

Global Faith Forum. "Bob Roberts Jr." *Global Faith Forum*. Accessed February 11, 2011. http://www.globalfaithforum.org/about/bob-roberts-jr.

Goldman, Russell. "Who Is Terry Jones? Pastor Behind 'Burn a Koran Day.'" *abc NEWS/U.S.* September 7, 2010. Accessed September 8, 2010. http://abcnews.go.com/US/terry-jones-pastor-burn-koran-day/story?id=11575665.

Grace and Truth Exposition. 2005. Accessed May 24, 2016. grace-truth.info/exposition/.

"Grace and Truth: Toward Christlike Relationships with Muslims: An Affirmation." Accessed May 24, 2016. http://www.ricklove.net/wp-content/uploads/2010/04/grace-and-truth-affirmation.pdf.

Guder, Darrell L., ed. *Missional Church: A Vision for the Sending of the Church in North America*. Grand Rapids: Eerdmans, 1998.

Gushee, David P. *The Sacredness of Human Life: Why an Ancient Biblical Vision is Key to the World's Future*. Grand Rapids: Eerdmans, 2013.

Works Cited

Hagberg, Janet O., and Robert A. Guelich. *The Critical Journey: Stages in the Life of Faith.* Salem: Sheffield, 2005.

Hagner, Donald A. *Word Biblical Commentary: Matthew 1–13,* 33A. Electronic edition. Dallas: Word, 2002.

"Heather Mercer and Dayna Curry Profile." Accessed January 16, 2015. www.cnn.com/CNN/Programs/people/shows/curry.mercer/profile.html.

Heideman, Eugene. "The Missiological Significance of the Universal Declaration of Human Rights." *Missiology: An International Review* XXVII.2 (2000) 164.

Hertz, Todd. *Opinion Roundup: Are Evangelicals the "New Internationalists?."* May 1, 2001. Accessed February 18, 2011. http://www.christianitytoday.com/ct/2002/mayweb-only/21.0.html.

Hock, Ronald F. "Paul's Tentmaking and the Problem of His Social Class." *Journal of Biblical Literature* 97 (1978) 555–64.

———. *The Social Context of Paul's Mission.* Philadelphia: Fortress, 1980.

———. "The Workshop as a Social Setting for Paul's Missionary Preaching." *The Catholic Biblical Quarterly* (1979) 438–50.

Hubbard, David Allen. *Thessalonians: Life That's Radically Christian.* Waco, TX: Word, 1977.

Institute for Spiritual Formation. Accessed January 16, 2015. www.talbot.edu.isf/.

Jeremias, Joachim. *Jerusalem in the Time of Jesus.* Philadelphia: Fortress, 1969.

Johnson, Neal C. *Business as Mission: A Comprehensive Guide to Theory and Practice.* Downers Grove, IL: InterVarsity Academic, 2009.

Johnstone, Patrick. *The Future of the Global Church: History, Trends and Possibilities.* Downers Grove, IL: InterVarsity, 2011.

Jones, Stanley. *The Christ of the Indian Road.* New York: Abingdon, 1925.

Kaiser, Walter C., Jr. *Toward an Old Testament Theology.* Grand Rapids: Zondervan, 1978.

Katangole, Emmanuel, and Chris Rice. *Reconciling All Things: A Christian Vision for Justice, Peace and Healing.* Downers Grove, IL: InterVarsity, 2008.

Katangole, Emmanuel, with Jonathan Wilson. *Mirror to the Church: Resurrecting Faith after Genocide in Rwanda.* Downers Grove, IL: InterVarsity, 2009.

Keener, Craig S. *The IVP Bible Background Commentary: New Testament.* Downers Grove, IL: InterVarsity, 1994.

Keller, Tim. *Characteristics of a Missional Church.* Desiring God 2006 National Conference. Accessed February 18, 2011. http://www.youtube.com/watch?v=zFFlSb-Zsc8.

———. *Generous Justice: How God's Grace Makes Us Just.* New York: Riverhead, 2012.

———. "Missional_Church-keller.pdf." *download.redeemer.com.* June, 2001. Accessed February 18, 2011. http://download.redeemer.com/pdf/learn/resources/Missional_Church-Keller.pdf.

Kemeny, P. C., ed. *Church, State, and Public Justice.* Downers Grove, IL: InterVarsity, 2007.

Kistemaker, Simon J. *1 Corinthians.* Grand Rapids: Baker, 1977.

Krafft, Steve. "Coca-Cola Controversy: 'America the Beautiful' Super Bowl ad draws criticism." Fox 10, Phoenix. February 3, 2014. Accessed January 10, 2015. http://www.fox10phoenix.com/story/24623870/2014/02/03/controversial-coca-cola-ad-hits-the-wrong-note-with-some-viewers.

Kristof, Nicholas D. "Following God Abroad." May 21, 2002. Accessed February 18, 2011. http://www.nytimes.com/2002/05/21/opinion/following-god-abroad.html.

———. "Learning From the Sin of Sodom." February 27, 2010. Accessed February 18, 2011. http://www.nytimes.com/2010/02/28/opinion/28kristof.html.

Works Cited

Lai, Patrick, and Rick Love. "An Integrated Identity in a Globalized World." In *From Seed to Fruit*, edited by J. Dudley Woodberry, 337–53. Pasadena, CA: William Carey Library, 2008.

The Lausanne Movement. *The Cape Town Commitment: A Confession of Faith and a Call to Action*. October 24, 2010. Accessed February 18, 2011. http://www.lausanne.org/ctcommitment.

Longenecker, Richard N. *Word Biblical Commentary: Galatians*. Vol. 41. Electronic edition. Dallas: Word, 1998.

———. *New Testament Social Ethics for Today*. Grand Rapids: Eerdmans, 1984.

Love, Fran. *Companion on the Journey*. Accessed January 16, 2015. www.franlove.com/.

Love, Rick. *Biblical Language and Military Metaphors: Sticks and Stones Revisited*. Pasadena, CA: Consultation on Mission Language and Metaphors, 2000. http://ricklove.net/?page_id=1646.

———. "Common Grace, Common Ground, and the Common Good, Part 1." February 13, 2012. peace-catalyst.net/blog/post/common-grace—common-ground—and-the-common-good—part-1-.

———. "Common Grace, Common Ground, and the Common Good, Part 2." February 16, 2012. peace-catalyst.net/blog/post/common-grace—common-ground—common-good—part-2-.

———. "Conversion, Respectful Witness and Freedom of Religion." April 12, 2010. Accessed February 11, 2011. http://ricklove.net/wp-content/uploads/2010/05/Lubar-Institute-Presentation-on-Conversion.pdf.

———. *Grace and Truth: Toward Christlike Relationships with Muslims*. Arvada, CO: Peace Catalyst International, 2013.

———. "Media and Violence: Reflections of an Aspiring Peacemaker." *ricklove.net*. May 13, 2008. Accessed February 18, 2011. http://www.ricklove.net/wp-content/uploads/2010/04/Media-and-Violence.pdf.

———. *Peace Catalysts: Resolving Conflict in Our Families, Organizations, and Communities*. Downers Grove, IL: InterVarsity, 2014.

———. "Rick Love Responds to Piper's Thoughts on a Common Word." January 28, 2008. Accessed May 22, 2016. www.desiringgod.org/blog/posts/rick-love-responds-to-pipers-thoughts-on-a-common-word.

"Loving God and Neighbor in Word and Deed." July 17, 2008. Accessed May 23, 2016. http://www.acommonword.com/loving-god-and-neighbor-in-word-and-deed-implications-for-christians-and-muslims/.

Lyons, Gabe. *The Next Christians: How a New Generation is Restoring the Faith*. New York: Doubleday, 2010.

Mafico, T. L. J. "Just, Justice." In *The Anchor Yale Bible Dictionary*, vol. 3, edited by D. N. Freedman, 1129. New York: Doubleday, 1992.

Martin Institute and Willard Center. Accessed January 16, 2015. www.westmont.edu/willard-center/.

"Martin Luther." *Wikipedia*. January 11, 2015. https://en.wikipedia.org/wiki/Martin_Luther.

Marty, Martin. *When Faiths Collide*. Malden, MA: Blackwell, 2005.

McGee, Gary Z. "Five Ways Those Who Love Peace Can Organize as Effectively as Those Who Love War." *Fractal Enlightenment*. Accessed May 2, 2017. https://fractalenlightenment.com/28127/life/5-ways-those-who-love-peace-can-organize-as-effectively-as-those-who-love-war.

Works Cited

McKnight, Scot. "Original Meaning." In *NIV Application Commentary, New Testament: Galatians*, 199. Grand Rapids: Zondervan, 1995.

MDiv with a Concentration in Christian Formation and Soul Care. Accessed August 7, 2015. www.denverseminary.edu/academics/master-of-divinity/christian-formation-soul-care.

Medearis, Carl. "The Myth of 'Love the Sinner Hate the Sin.'" October 10, 2011. peace-catalyst.net/blog/post/carl-medearis:—the-myth-of-love-the-sinner—hate-the-sin.

———. *Muslims, Christians, and Jesus: Gaining Understanding and Building Relationships*. Grand Rapids: Bethany House, 2008.

———. *Speaking of Jesus*. Colorado Springs: David C. Cook, 2011.

Metzger, Bruce M. *A Textual Commentary on the Greek New Testament*. 4th. New York: United Bible Societies, 2001.

"Missional Living." *Wikipedia*. Accessed February 18, 2011. http://en.wikipedia.org/wiki/Missional_living#The_missional_church.

Moghul, Haroon. "Jesus Carpet Bomb my Heart: An Undercover Muslim in Detroit." March 19, 2012. http://religiondispatches.org/jesus-carpet-bomb-my-heart-an-undercover-muslim-in-detroit/.

Montefiore, C. G. and H. Loewe, eds. *A Rabbinic Anthology*. New York: Schocken, 1974.

Moore, Russell L. *Onward: Engaging the Culture without Losing the Gospel*. Nashville: B&H, 2015.

Murray, Stuart. *The Naked Anabaptist: The Bare Essentials of a Radical Faith*. Scottdale, PA: Herald, 2010.

Name Withheld. Personal Correspondence with the Author. 2003.

"The New Colossus." *Wikipedia*. November 22, 2014. en.wikipedia.org/wiki/The_New_Colossus.

NIV Application Commentary, New Testament: Ephesians. Grand Rapids: Zondervan, 1996.

Norman, Steve. "Pastors and the Peacemaking Paradox." August 21, 2013. peace-catalyst.net/blog.post/pastors-and-the-peacemaking-paradox.

Open Doors. Accessed January 17, 2015. bit.ly/1i1YJET.

Partlow, Joshua. "Protests over Koran Burning Spread in Afghanistan, with 9 Dead in Kandahar." *The Washington Post*. April 2, 2011.. Accessed January 10, 2015. http://www.washingtonpost.com/world/taliban-attack-nato-base-in-kabul-koran-protests-spread/2011/04/02/AFTC9rMC_story.html.

"Pastors Reject Apology Order over Koran Comments." *ABCNewsOnline*. June 22, 2005. Accessed February 18, 2011. http://www.abc.net.au/news/newsitems/200506/s1397914.htm.

Patel, Eboo. "The Faith Divide: From Fearing Islam to Loving Muslims." *On Faith at washingtonpost.com*. November 17, 2010. Accessed February 18, 2011. http://onfaith.washingtonpost.com/onfaith/eboo_patel/2010/11/converting_america.html.

Ramsbotham, Oliver, Tom Woodhouse and Hugh Miall. *Contemporary Conflict Resolution*. 2nd ed. Cambridge: Polity, 2005.

"Redeemer Presbyterian Church." Accessed February 18, 2011. http://www.redeemer.com/.

Roberts, Bob, Jr. *Bold as Love: What Can Happen When People See People the Way God Does*. Nashville: Thomas Nelson, 2012.

———. *Glocalization: How Followers of Jesus Engage the New Flat World*. Grand Rapids: Zondervan, 2007.

Works Cited

———. *Real-Time Connections: Linking Your Job with God's Global Work.* Grand Rapids: Zondervan, 2010.
Rupp, George. "Sending, Receiving, Embracing: The Pulse of Global Immigration." *Reflections: Yale Divinity School* (2008) 23.
Russell, Mark L. *The Missional Entrepreneur.* Birmingham, AL: New Hope, 2010.
Ryken, Leland, James Wilhoit, Tremper Longman, C. Duriez, D. Penney, and D. G. Reid. *Dictionary of Biblical Imagery.* Electronic edition. Downers Grove, IL: InterVarsity, 2000.
Sanders, Doug. *The Myth of the Muslim Tide: Do Immigrants Threaten the West.* New York: Vintage, 2012.
"San Diego County, California." *Wikipedia.* January 9. Accessed January 10, 2015. http://en.wikipedia.org/wiki/San_Diego_County,_California#Demographics.
Seiple, Chris. "Christian Mission in Every Sphere." February 25, 2011. globalengage.org/news-media/from-the-president/christian-mission-in-every-sphere.
Seiple, Robert A. "From Bible Bombardment to Incarnational Evangelism: A Reflection on Christian Witness and Persecution." *The Review of Faith and International Affairs* 7.1 (2009) 29–38.
Shahid, Aliyah, and Corky Siemaszko. "President Obama takes on preacher Terry Jones and controversial plan for Sept. 11 Koran burn." *NYDailyNews.* September 10, 2010. Accessed September 12, 2010. http://www.nydailynews.com/news/national/2010/09/10/2010-09-10_pastor_terry_jones_goes_on_morning_media_blitz_clarifies_little_about_burning_ko.html.
Shenk, David. "Three Journeys: Jesus—Constantine—Muhammad." http://s3.amazonaws.com/churchplantmedia-cms/peacecatalyst_az/three-journeys-david-shenk-article.pdf.
Sieff, Kevin. "Florida pastor Terry Jones' Koran burning has far reaching effect." April 2, 2011. www.washingtonpost.com/local/education/florida-pastor-terry-joness-koran-burning-has-far-reaching-effect/2011/04/02/AFpiFoQC_story.html.
Siemens, Ruth E. "Tentmakers Needed for World Evangelization." In *Perspectives on the World Christian Movement*, edited by Ralph Winter and Steven C. Hawthorne, 737. Pasadena, CA: William Carey Library, 1999.
Southwestern Baptist Theological Seminary. "Taking the Hill." *Southwestern Baptist Theological Seminary.* Accessed February 18, 2011. http://www.swbts.edu/takingthehill.
Stark, Rodney. *For the Glory of God: How Monotheism Led to Reformations, Science, Witch Hunts, and the End of Slavery.* Princeton, NJ: Princeton University Press, 2004.
———. *The Rise of Christianity: How the Obscure, Marginal Jesus Movement Became the Dominant Religious Force in the Western World in a Few Centuries.* San Francisco: Harper Collins, 1997.
Stetzer, Ed. "A Missional Church." *The Christian Index.* October 13, 2005. Accessed February 18, 2011. http://www.christianindex.org/1657.article.
Stott, John. *Human Rights and Human Wrongs.* Grand Rapids: Baker, 1999.
———. *The Message of Galatians (Bible Speaks Today).* Vol. 109. Downers Grove, IL: InterVarsity, 1968.
Swanson, Eric, and Sam Williams. *To Transform a City: Whole Church, Whole Gospel, Whole City.* Grand Rapids: Zondervan, 2010.
Talbert, Charles H. *Reading Acts: A Literary and Theological Commentary on the Acts of the Apostles.* New York: Crossroad, 1997.

Works Cited

Tate, M. E. "Psalms 51–100." In *Word Biblical Commentary*. Electronic edition, Logos Library System. Dallas: Word, 1998.

Tennett, Timothy. "Being a 'Glocal' Preacher." *Global Talk*. October 5, 2009. Accessed February 11, 2011. http://blogs.asburyseminary.edu/global-talk/being-a-glocal-preacher/.

Thiessen, Elmer John. *The Ethics of Evangelism: A Philosophical Defense of Proselytizing and Persuasion*. Downers Grove, IL: InterVarsity, 2011.

Turner, David L. *Matthew*. Grand Rapids: Baker Academic, 2008.

The Universal Declaration of Human Rights. December 10, 1948. Accessed January 17, 2015. http://www.un.org/en/universal-declaration-human-rights/index.html.

Vaughan, Curtis. "Colossians/V. Appeal for Christian Living (3:1–4:6)/B. Guidelines for the Christian Life (3:5–4:6)/b. The duty of witnessing (4:5, 6)." In *The Expositor's Bible Commentary: Pradis CD-ROM: Colossians Version 4.0.2*, edited by Frank E. Gaebelein. Zondervan.

Veith, Gene Edward, Jr. *God at Work*. Wheaton, IL: Crossway, 2002.

Venter, Alexander. *Doing Reconciliation: Racism, Reconciliation and Transformation in the Church and World*. Cape Town, South Africa: Vineyard International, 2004.

Vineyard USA. Accessed May 25, 2016. http://www.vineyardusa.org/.

Vineyard Columbus. VineyardColumbus.org. Accessed February 18, 2011. http://vineyardcolumbus.org/.

Waldman, Steven. *Founding Faith: How our Founding Fathers Forged a Radical New Approach to Religious Liberty*. New York: Random House, 2008.

"Why do we Share the Good News About Jesus with all Peoples, Including Muslims?" *Ricklove.net*. Accessed January 18, 2015. http://www.ricklove.net/wp-content/uploads/2010/04/Why-we-share-the-good-news-with-Muslims.pdf.

Winter, Ralph. "Four Men, Three Eras." Accessed May 23, 2016. https://www.frontiermissionfellowship.org/uploads/documents/Four%20Men%20Three%20Eras.pdf.

Woodberry, J. Dudley. "Toward Mutual Respectful Witness." In *Peace-Building By, Between, and Beyond Muslims and Evangelical Christians*, edited by David Augsburger and Abu-Nimer, 171–178. Lanham, MD: Lexington, 2009.

Wright, Christopher J. H. *The Mission of God: Unlocking the Bible's Grand Narrative*. Downers Grove, IL: InterVarsity Academic, 2006.

Wright, N. T. *Evil and the Justice of God*. Downers Grove, IL: InterVarsity, 2006.

Wunderink, Susan. "You've Got Jail: Missionaries' imprisonment shows the security risks of support e-mails." *Christianity Today*. February 17, 2009. Accessed February 18, 2011. http://www.christianitytoday.com/ct/2009/march/8.14.html.

www.ingramcontent.com/pod-product-compliance
Lightning Source LLC
Chambersburg PA
CBHW020854160426
43192CB00007B/919